Rabbi Charles H. Middleburgh

The Prophets of Israel

A Sideways View

Hadassa Word Press

Impressum / Imprint
Bibliografische Information der Deutschen Nationalbibliothek: Die Deutsche Nationalbibliothek verzeichnet diese Publikation in der Deutschen Nationalbibliografie; detaillierte bibliografische Daten sind im Internet über http://dnb.d-nb.de abrufbar.

Bibliographic information published by the Deutsche Nationalbibliothek: The Deutsche Nationalbibliothek lists this publication in the Deutsche Nationalbibliografie; detailed bibliographic data are available in the Internet at http://dnb.d-nb.de.

Coverbild / Cover image: www.ingimage.com

Verlag / Publisher:
Hadassa Word Press
ist ein Imprint der / is a trademark of
OmniScriptum GmbH & Co. KG
Bahnhofstraße 28, 66111 Saarbrücken, Deutschland / Germany
Email: info@omniscriptum.com

Herstellung: siehe letzte Seite /
Printed at: see last page
ISBN: 978-3-639-79519-6

Dedication

To my treasured students
Daniel, Danny, Haim, Hannah, Kath, Naomi, and Robyn,
the class of 2017,
whose enthusiasm, creativity and enjoyment has raised my passion for the
Prophets to fresh heights

For my beloved Gilly
who has been telling me for ages to sit down and write a book

and

My wonderful friends Elaina and Gerald Rothman
whose gracious and matchless hospitality
gave me the head and heart space to write

CONTENTS

Introduction 1

Early Prophets

Chapter 1   Miriam and Deborah 7

Chapter 2   Samuel 11

Chapter 3   Nathan and Huldah 16

Chapter 4   Ahijah, Micaiah, and Elijah 22

Chapter 5   Elisha 29

Major Prophets

Chapter 6   Isaiah: 1, 2 & 3 35

Chapter 7   Jeremiah 45

Chapter 8   Ezekiel 59

Minor Prophets

Chapter 9   Twelve Minor Prophets 67

    I   Hosea 67

    II   Joel 69

    III   Amos 71

    VI   Obadiah 75

    V   Jonah 77

    VI   Micah 81

    VII   Nahum 85

    VIII   Habakkuk 87

    IX   Zephaniah 90

    X   Haggai 92

    XI   Zechariah 93

    XII   Malachi 97

Chapter 10   Daniel 100

Postscript 103

Glossary 104

Suggestions for further reading 106

Notes 107

About the Author 113

Introduction

I have served as a congregational rabbi for many years. Throughout that time at Sabbath and Festival services I have heard a reading from the Prophetic books of the Hebrew Bible, read as a *haftarah*, a complementary reading to one from the Torah (the five Books of Moses) that preceded it.

I would look out at my congregants and see them struggling to understand what they were hearing and what, if any, relevance it might have to their own lives. Many of these selections were ages old, having been specified by rabbinic sages in Babylon during the Talmudic period; so I worked on a new lectionary for the Liberal Jews of the United Kingdom, one of whose rabbis I was, removing some of the worst offenders from the traditional list and replacing them with readings that were more appropriate and uplifting.

However, the die was cast. For me, and many of my colleagues, the *haftarah* is embedded as a 'switch off' point in the minds of our congregants, a warm up possibly for the major 'switch off' of the service, the rabbi's sermon, which follows shortly afterwards!

Throughout this time I was teaching various biblical texts to my students at Leo Baeck College, often prophetic books such as Isaiah and Amos, but it was only recently, in 2012, that I created a new module called *The Prophets*. It is a two semester course, enabling the students to study a selection of material about prophets great and small, to get under their skin and, hopefully, pick up my enthusiasm for the genre and take that enthusiasm to the congregations they will serve.

My teaching of the Hebrew Bible has been subconsciously informed at all times by a response to one key image, that of the white gloves of an antiquarian librarian carefully opening a precious manuscript. The idea that the Hebrew Bible, because of its antiquity and singular importance in Jewish life and tradition, has to be handled with white gloves and spoken about in soft tones is anathema to me. Why? Certainly not because of lack of love for the text – to study it is one of my chief joys – nor disrespect, but because I know that my Hebrew Bible is a tough text that can handle the most robust of treatments.

I also know that entering the study of the Prophets with an ancient heart and a modern eye is to give them and the material that bears their names more than enough respect. The combination of love and eager questioning informed by the worlds in which I live brings forth hidden gems from the texts under analysis, leading to new ideas and teachings which make the Prophets more rather than less relevant to those who wish to live a modern life informed by and infused with a religious tradition.

Defining prophecy is not as easy as it sounds. Is the authentic sign of a prophet, as stipulated by Moses in the book of Deuteronomy, that what they pronounce actually occurs? Or is the crucial factor that those named as prophets stood out from the crowd because God not only talked to them but through them? The Mosaic definition might well exclude some of the prophets whose books occur in the Bible, and others seem to have used language the ambiguity of which leaves it hard for the reader to decide whether the events referred to have already happened or are about to happen.

In oracles where a prophet denounces a particular city or country and prophesies their doom, a quite common occurrence, whatever their prophetic skills may have been I have always believed that they were well plugged into events within and beyond their own countries and felt able to take a punt based on what was likely to happen, and inevitably in some cases got it right.

Why also we must ask was prophetic activity in the Hebrew Bible purely within the monarchic period, from the eleventh to the sixth centuries BCE? For me, at least, the answer is clear.

The Kings of Israel and Judah, whatever their cultic roles, needed to practice *realpolitik*, often blurring or crossing the edges of prophetic morality.

In addition, the period of the biblical monarchy and that of the Temple in Jerusalem are almost identical, and it is unlikely that the priests, whose need for political stability was important, were able to detach themselves from the king on whom they depended. So with monarchy and priesthood joined in an unholy if pragmatic nexus a moral void was left which needed to be filled, and it was into this void that the prophets stepped, showing neither fear nor favour to either.

The prominence and teaching of the biblical prophets was extremely influential in early Christianity, and in the Christian Bible there is more than one assertion that key events and figures in the gospels were fulfilling one or other prophecy of a Hebrew prophet [Matthew 3.1–3]; and the influence of Hebrew biblical teachings and individuals in early Islam, through *israilyat* in the Qur'an and the Hadith, was considerable. It cannot be accidental that the title of the man who founded the Islamic religion is not king, or emperor, or high priest, but prophet.

A modern Jewish perception, informed by rabbinic teachings, may be that prophecy became extinct at the end of the biblical period, but I believe it would be wrong to think so.

Every age has its prophets, men and women who stand for changes that society may not readily embrace but ultimately do so under the force of the prophet's arguments; or they may lead a religious movement which has a transformative effect on their country, or even beyond; or they may stand against injustice, at home and abroad, and grow so much in stature that their thoughts and their ideas cannot be ignored.

It is perhaps easy to see the rabbinic closure of the age of prophecy as motivated more by pragmatism than philosophy; once Jewish life was largely dictated by rabbinic law (the *halakhah*) it was the rabbis who became the universal arbiters of all things. They became the establishment and having done so they realised that there could no longer be a place for those whose role was principally to kick against the status quo and denounce it. So they drew a line – prophecy ended with Malachi – and thus did rabbinic Judaism eclipse prophetic Judaism, until the latter was 'rediscovered' by the early Reformers of Judaism in the 19th century.

However, just as there is good religion and bad religion so there are good and bad prophets. How they are categorised may well be dictated by the attitudes of their time, and accepted norms of public discourse.

The biblical prophets inveigh against the enemies of Israel in language that their audiences would probably have appreciated but which grate on or even embarrass us: so what should our response be?

It is always misguided to judge an earlier time by contemporary standards, so some allowances should be made, and although we should not seek to whitewash the *Sturm und Drang* mixed into some otherwise sublime and uplifting language, we should not allow the latter to be diminished by the former as we read prophetic material.

I have subtitled this book *A Sideways View*, to indicate that I would try and approach the text, where appropriate, in a more lateral way than is conventionally the case, and through that approach to mine fresh gems from the material. I take this approach, extracting from the biblical material whatever it yields not out of lack of respect, but because my love of the Hebrew Bible demands of me that I share my enthusiasm with others.

You will not find Abraham or Moses written about in this book, though each is called a prophet by the Torah and each transmits God's word and intercedes with God (key prophetic criteria). I have excluded them because the function of each is much more complex, and neither fits easily with the template of the greats of Israelite prophecy.

My goal in this book is the same as for my teaching, communication with those I teach, so it is my sincere hope that members of all three of the Abrahamic traditions, and those of another faith or none, will read this book, and will find within its pages material that makes them think and question and perhaps find their own way into the extraordinary literary genres of the Hebrew Bible.

Charles Middleburgh
Leo Baeck College
January 2017
Tevet 5777

EARLY PROPHETS

Chapter 1

Miriam and Deborah

Key texts: Exodus 15.20; Numbers 12.2; Judges 4.4
Dates: ca. 14th–12th centuries BCE

There are many approaches to the biblical text, and it has been said recently by several scholars that the field is so overcrowded that it is almost impossible to ascertain which, if any, is the most valid. For the purpose of this book I am taking a chronological or 'eye-level view', following the Bible's own chronology, and the first person in the Hebrew Bible to be labelled a prophet by the text*[1] is, surprisingly perhaps, a woman. In Exodus 15, following the crossing of the Sea of Reeds and after Moses has lead the Israelites in the Song of the Sea, Miriam and the women of Israel gather together and, accompanied by musical instruments, chant one stanza of the Song; it is here that she is call *ha-neviah*, the prophetess.[i]

Now there's quite a lot going on in this part of Exodus: the Israelites have just trekked through the Sea of Reeds and then witnessed the pursuing Egyptians destroyed when the waters that had parted for them crashed together. They have been liberated from slavery; they are at the start of the long and challenging road to the covenant with God at Mt Sinai. In this plethora of detail it is all too easy to ignore one little word, *ha-neviah*, and miss something powerful.

---

*In speaking of Abraham to King Abimelech of Gerar, God inflates the patriarch's importance by calling him 'navi', a prophet [Gen 20.7], defining him so because he 'can intercede'; I see this as good PR rather than a proper designation, unlike Miriam who carries it as a respectful title.

I always teach my students that it is not just enough to know what the words of the Hebrew Bible mean, or to understand the grammar, it is necessary to question **everything**. Why is the text framed as it is? Why are the specific words in a given verse used? Is there a deeper truth below the immediate meaning? Do the meanings of cognate words in other Semitic languages shed further light on the Hebrew text?

Taking this approach doesn't always yield startling results (though it does so regularly), but by having this robust relationship with the biblical text it may even be possible to derive meanings that have by-passed the greatest of biblical commentators throughout Jewish history. What is also achieved is the injection of dynamism into Bible study which refreshes and invigorates teacher and student alike.

Let us return to Miriam. Why might she be called 'the prophetess'? If we judge on the basis of standard definitions of the verb to prophesy – to utter prophecies, to speak prophetically, to foretell the future [Chambers, 11th edition, p.1246] – then the title doesn't seem to fit at all. The definition of the noun prophecy helps a little – 'an inspired or prophetic utterance, a prediction' – but doesn't really seal the deal. If we turn to a Hebrew dictionary we don't get much more help, although the classic *Brown Driver Briggs Hebrew and English Lexicon of the Old Testament*, BDB to generations of bible students, gives an interesting hint when it offers for the Hebrew verb form 'religious ecstasy with or without song or music' [BDB p.612]. However, to my lateral eye, that definition may be derived from the juxtaposition of 'the prophetess' with a context of song and dance in Exodus 15.20, which only serves to lead us round in a circle.

Help, however, may be at hand in the book of Numbers, where a family row erupts between Aaron and Miriam and their brother Moses: the latter has remarried and, as often happens in families, the siblings don't approve.[ii] Picking a fight with their brother who had God as his special friend was not a wise move, as both discover. When they are chuntering away to each other they say, 'Has the Lord spoken only through Moses? Has he not spoken through us as well?'

Now as we know, those people in the Bible through whom God speaks are most commonly designated 'prophets', so perhaps this text influenced the Exodus verse and gave rise to Miriam being given the title 'prophetess'? Yet how could that be when Numbers comes *after* Exodus in the canon? Scholars who espouse the famous Documentary Hypothesis of biblical criticism, positing the presence of at least four major strands from different periods, may have an answer, for it is suggested that both the Exodus and the Numbers texts are from the same strand [E].

This still leaves us with the question as to why Miriam is called 'the prophetess'. An answer may well be that if both our texts are contemporaneous and neither influenced the other, the title arose from an understanding by the writers that because Moses and Aaron were as important as they were, their sister could not in her own way have been less special, and so they accorded her the title of prophetess to indicate that fact.

The rabbis seem to have been just as puzzled by Miriam's title as the rest of us and in the *Midrash Rabbah*, the great text of rabbinic biblical exegesis, they explain it by saying that she prophesied while still a child that her mother would bear a son who would save his people.[iii] Noting that in the Exodus text she is described as the sister of Aaron, rather than the sister of Aaron *and* Moses, they suggest that she deserved the title because she prophesied Moses' birth before it had occurred! While exemplifying the challenges faced by the rabbis in understanding the full meaning of some biblical texts, such stories add colour rather than substance to the biblical narrative.

If Miriam being designated 'the prophetess' in the Hebrew Bible is intriguing and puzzling, how much the more so is the case of Deborah who was given the same title.

Deborah is found in the book of Judges, the leading protagonists of which bear the title of Judge. The pattern of behaviour that brings a 'judge' to the fore is that the people of Israel sin, and are disadvantaged by neighbouring tribes, so that in the end they cry out to God and a charismatic figure is inspired by the Divine Spirit to stand tall and lead them, initially in battle but later in the role of unifying figure and protector.

Some of the judges are among the most well-known characters in the Bible, Gideon, Jephthah and Samson to name but three: Deborah, however, is the only woman to fulfil this role although when she is first mentioned the text states 'she led Israel at that time' and acted as an arbiter for anyone who needed a decision or ruling. She is the only woman to lead the people until Queen Athaliah, and she usurped the throne! [9th century BCE], but is never given the title of judge, rather Deborah is called the 'prophetess'.

Why this is the case may be explained by the fact that she is the singer of a grand song of bloody triumph after the defeat of the forces of the king of Canaan, Yabin, in which she clearly played a part as the support and inspiration for her general Barak.[iv] The Song itself appears to have some echoes of the Exodus 15 text although its specifics and context are very different, and as this part of Judges at least is dated to the seventh century BCE, making it later than the Exodus extract, that influence is possible.

The real explanation for Deborah's title may be more prosaic however. In Judges 4.5[v] she is described as sitting under a palm tree bearing her name and giving advice and judgements to those who came to her for this purpose.

Then she summons Barak and tells him that the God of Israel has commanded him to attack the Canaanites and promises him victory. Communicating the divine word in the first person is a prophetic prerogative and thus Deborah's initially surprising title is shown to be not that surprising at all.

Deborah makes only a fleeting appearance in the Hebrew Bible, and the conquest of the Canaanites is led by Barak, not her, and their triumph is sealed not by Deborah but by another woman Yael, who murdered the fleeing Canaanite general Sisera.[vi]

Nevertheless, she is a significant figure in the chain of tradition wherein women could become popular leaders, and paved the way for later women in such roles.

Chapter 2

Samuel

Key texts: 1 Samuel 2.1-4.1; 7.2-13.15; 15.1-16.13; 25.1; 28.3-20
Dates: ca. 11th century BCE

There is little doubt that Samuel, sometimes labelled the last judge and first prophet, is a giant who bestrides the narrow pages that tell his story in the first of the two books that bear his name.

He started his life as a Temple acolyte at the shrine of Shiloh in the Canaanite hill country, a linen-clad youth ministering to the needs of the Temple's chief priest Eli. Eli, once a towering religious figure, is old and weak and his sons have already betrayed their priestly calling. Samuel is a miracle child, born to a long barren mother,[vii] and when she brings him to Shiloh as a gift to God and God talks to Samuel Eli quickly recognises that the boy is special. It would appear to be a promising start but life is to change Samuel in many ways, as it changes us all, and our last encounter with him does not just frighten it terrifies.

The first time God speaks to Samuel he pronounces the doom of Eli and his heirs, and all the subsequent predictions that Samuel makes come to fruition.[viii] As may be easily imagined this gives Samuel's reputation a mighty burnish and we are told that all Israel from north to south recognised that he was a true prophet and that God revealed himself to him at Shiloh.

Samuel is not a war leader like the judges before him, going into battle and routing Israel's enemies, indeed the battle that occurs immediately after his role as a prophet is stated is a disaster which results in the Philistines seizing the Ark of the Covenant, a huge blow. The prize was ultimately more trouble than it was worth to the Philistines and they returned it to the Israelite village of *Kiryat Ye-arim* where it was to stay for many years.[ix] For an extended period Samuel held his people together, sustaining them in times of crisis, invoking divine protection against the Philistines as long as he lived, and constantly visiting the key Israelite strongholds to act as a judge.

In spite of making a huge contribution to the stabilisation of his people and strengthening their hold on their land, as Samuel grows old and his sons, like Eli's, betray their calling and their father, the leaders of the people demand that he find them a king.[x]

This rejection by the tribes he had unified and for whom he had done so much, would have been a hurtful blow to Samuel, and he responds to the request in bitter tones pointing out all the things kings take from their peoples, from which the Israelites are currently free, and the dangers posed by an all-powerful human ruler.[xi] But it is no good. The Israelites want a king to make them the same as other nations and to lead them in battle. This is the crucial clincher, and God tells Samuel to do as the people have asked and find them a ruler.

Ironically, considering his expressed opposition to the institution, Samuel is to anoint two kings, Saul the charismatic but troubled Benjaminite, and David of the tribe of Judah, the golden boy-warrior who will found a dynasty.

Samuel's relationship with Saul is coloured by his antipathy to the idea of monarchy so, apart from the natural human reaction against being pensioned off after a lifetime of service especially when the replacement is young and full of vigour, perhaps there is an added dimension. Samuel has seen Eli brought low, his sons disgraced, and Samuel's own sons have behaved badly and let him down. Perhaps he sees the institution of monarchy as a framework which will see such bad apples potentially attain the throne and then wreak havoc from their position of power and privilege.

There is a rigid formality to the anointing of Saul, easily understood as a reflection of the fact that Samuel is acting out of necessity rather than choice.[xii] Samuel has a far greater appreciation of what Saul will be and what he will have to contend with than Saul himself, yet there are no words of encouragement nor any real blessing from Samuel, which could have been seen as a symbolic transfer of authority; he just anoints him in God's name, and assures him that God is with him, then sends him on his way.

This, however, proves to be the first of two coronations, the first having been private; in an age millennia before mass communication there had to be one in front of the masses. Saul seals his reputation by leading an army against the Ammonites, and it is in the wake of this victory that his public coronation takes place at the shrine of Gilgal. Yet the king himself stays silent and Samuel indulges in a long, and rather bitter, diatribe.[xiii]

Careful reading of the speech[xiv] suggests that this is a valedictory which, like many such addresses, contains a section of self-justification, another of self-aggrandisement, and a further bit of invective directed at his ungrateful people which God abets by sending down rain and thunder at Samuel's request.

Finally, Samuel tells the gathered tribes that although they have been wicked in God's eyes (by which he means his as well) he will continue to pray to God on their behalf. This sounds wonderful, but there is a definite sub-text which states – you know God listens to **me**, how do you know he will listen to your new king?

Sadly, for the rest of Saul's brief reign, Samuel is a thorn in his side. He has rarely begun before a miscalculation at a time of military threat leads him to perform a priestly function which Samuel criticises, adding that God has rejected him for not following the proper practice and will not allow him to father a dynasty.[xv] When Saul shows compassion to the King of the Amalekites, Israel's sworn enemies, and fails to fulfil Samuel's command to utterly destroy them and everything they have, Samuel damns him by stating that having rejected God's orders God has rejected him.[xvi]

Saul's pleas for clemency are met with stony rejection, and even when he abases himself and grabs the corner of Samuel's robe so that it tears, the prophet uses the torn piece of cloth as a metaphor for Saul's kingdom being torn from his hands. And, to complete his humiliation of Saul, Samuel by now an old man takes a sword and hacks the Amalekite king to death.

At this momentous point the two men part company and we are told that Samuel never saw Saul again, yet having returned home it seems that in the aftermath of all this tension and stress Samuel has second thoughts. Perhaps he had been too harsh with Saul? Perhaps he had judged him too quickly? Either way, he grieves over Saul and the mess that had been made of the reign of this first king of Israel in which he, Samuel, had played a prominent part. At this point God intervenes and directs Samuel to stop mourning and go and anoint another king, David son of Jesse, on which mission the old man sets out with some trepidation.

The final encounter between Saul and Samuel is the most terrifying, and troubling.[xvii]

Samuel has died and been buried in his home town. We are told that among the things that Saul had instigated was the persecution of necromancers. The Philistine threat has grown to its most menacing; a battle is inevitable and Saul has few options left.

His own mental torment is so severe that having persecuted witches and mediums he seeks out one of the last remaining, the witch of Endor, and in disguise asks her to summon from the dead someone whose name he will give her. Saul is unmasked and allays the witch's terror by promising her freedom from retribution if she does what he asks. Who does he summon? The ghost of Samuel!

The witch describes a divine being coming up from the earth, an old man wrapped in a robe, and Saul knows it is the ghost of Samuel. He grovels before him, a powerful act of obeisance for a king, but Samuel is unmoved. Frostily he asks why he has been summoned; the king's reply, his fear and desperate need for reassurance are in vain. Samuel confirms Saul's rejection by God, the fact that the kingship will pass to David, and then chillingly adds, 'Tomorrow, you and your sons will be with me'.[xviii]

Samuel's final exchange with Saul, icy and full of stony rejection, dramatizes not only the rupture in their relationship but also the lack of humanity that seems to characterise so much of Samuel's adult relationships, the hard unbending will of the self-righteous. Samuel demonstrates that even those to whom the Eternal speaks are not always elevated by this most privileged of dialogues.

Chapter 3

Nathan and Huldah*

Key texts: 2 Samuel 7; 12; 1 Kings 1. 32–36, 38, 39; 2 Kings 22.14–20
Dates: Nathan – ca. 1000 BCE
      Huldah – 7th century BCE

Thanks to Georg Frederic Handel, almost everyone knows that 'Zadok the Priest and Nathan the Prophet anointed Solomon king'. If you search for this precise phrase in the first chapter of the first book of Kings you will be disappointed for Handel brought elements of three verses together to link to one of his most famous pieces of music. Thankfully, we know much more about Nathan than his involvement in Solomon's coronation.

We first encounter Nathan in the second book of Samuel, in conversation with King David about building a temple for God, which Nathan encourages him to do.[xix] Unfortunately, we know nothing of Nathan's origins or rise to prominence, he appears fully formed at the king's side; perhaps when the text was written Nathan was so well known that the writer did not need to add more detail, equally this could just be another infuriating biblical gap that was never filled in.

Then again, perhaps the back story was unimportant as it was his role with the first two kings of a united kingdom of Israel that mattered. At David's side Nathan encourages him to follow his intentions about building a house for God but, a little later, when the word of God has come to him explaining that God seeks no temple from David but will rather wait till the reign of his

---

*Although Huldah dates to the time of Jeremiah I have included her here because, like Nathan, she is a significant prophetic figure but not of the stature or importance of her more famous contemporary.

heir, Nathan, in God's name, softens the blow by promising David that his renown will last forever and his dynasty will be sustained by God.[xx]

Nathan is shown here not just to be a mouthpiece but a man of great sensitivity; that he succeeds in giving David disappointing news without devastating him is proved by David's response, a torrent of praise to God pours from his mouth, as well as a repeat of key planks of the promise just in case God has a memory lapse!

A few chapters later, the role played by Nathan is very different and much more challenging.

David has started an affair with a woman married to one of his soldiers, a Hittite warrior called Uriah.

One imagines that the king could have had any woman he desired, married or not, but with Bathsheba David is aflame; he doesn't just want sex he wants ownership.

It is the way he goes about this that brings him into conflict with Nathan the prophet: for David gives orders that Uriah is to be in the front rank at the next battle and when the enemy attacks his comrades are to allow him to be overwhelmed; and as the king desires so is it accomplished. In his eagerness to have Bathsheba to himself he has her brought to his palace immediately after her formal mourning for her husband is over, and the next thing we know she is pregnant and gives birth to a son.

David must have thought he was home and dry, having successfully manipulated his way through all the obstacles that stood between him and Bathsheba, now his wife. He is about to discover, however, just how wrong he was.

God is deeply displeased and sends Nathan to see David. The text does not indicate that he was given a set of words to repeat, rather that it was left to him to find the right approach.

Nathan reveals himself to be a man of enormous subtlety and courage, willing to speak truth to power even when it might bring him into conflict with David whom he must have loved, and who might have returned that feeling, were he not challenged by Nathan's behaviour.

He asks David for advice on a case that has come to his attention. A wealthy shepherd, whose flocks and herds were plentiful, had coveted the single lamb of a poor man and had then taken it from him to serve to a guest, rather than use one of his own. The king is outraged!

'Who is this man?' he roars, 'he deserves to be punished four times over for this terrible crime!' And Nathan, quietly but devastatingly replies, 'You are the rich man'. To make matters even worse he delivers the rest in the words of God, a judgement from which David cannot escape.

In Nathan's mouth God is disgusted with David's behaviour, accusing him of base ingratitude for all the great things that God has gifted him; to take another man's wife and then have the man killed is despicable and a price must be paid. And the price is terrible. Because David's sin concerned another man's wife, his own wives will be dishonoured in public and his house will be riven with strife.[xxi]

The effectiveness of Nathan's approach and the power of his message is proved by David's response; no excuses, no attempts at exculpation, he just says, in two succinct Hebrew words, *Chatati ladonai,* 'I have sinned before the Lord'. Just as suddenly as he has devastated David, Nathan reassures him that he shall not die for his sin – the punishment David wanted to inflict on the rich man in Nathan's parable – but another will die, his and Bathsheba's first child.[xxii]

There is nothing to suggest that Nathan and David have any significant dealings after this incredibly tense meeting, perhaps there was a short estrangement, perhaps David just felt too guilty to see his spiritual mentor, but that they are reconciled is shown by the fact that after Bathsheba gives birth to her second child who she names Solomon, God sends Nathan to tell the happy couple that God has given him a second name, *Yedid-yah,* meaning beloved of the Lord.[xxiii]

This is the last we hear of Nathan in second Samuel although a prophet called Gad, named as David's seer [2.S.24.11], about whom we otherwise know nothing, is inspired by God to give David an oracle at a time of crisis as a result of which he sets up an altar on the threshing floor of Araunah the Jebusite, the place where Solomon's temple will ultimately be built.

Just why it is Gad and not Nathan who delivers this message is puzzling and he is similarly absent in the retelling of the incident in Chronicles [1.Chron.21]. The rabbis seem to have been intrigued by the mystery of Gad's origins and his single appearance on the Davidic stage, referring to him once as part of a select gathering with David and Nathan [Exod.R. 15.20], though they delineate his status clearly as a 'seer', 'one who sees', rather than a prophet like Nathan, one who communicates the word of God.

Nathan's final role in David's life occurs when the king is on his deathbed and a crisis erupts over who will succeed him.

It is unsurprising that Nathan, who had previously given the name 'Beloved of the Lord' to Solomon, steps in to mobilise the power of those behind Solomon, including his father and mother, which leads directly to the anointing of Solomon by Zadok with Nathan either in close attendance or sharing the act of anointing (both are implied).

And that appears to be that, but for one final reference [1.K.4.5] to the two sons of Nathan indicating that they were part of Solomon's inner circle, a further testimony to the huge importance of Nathan in the reign of King David and, precisely when it counted, the reign of his son Solomon.

Although Nathan is arguably most widely known thanks to Handel it is for his role as the speaker of truth to power, when he castigates David for his cupidity but in a manner that brings about repentance rather than destruction, that he should be remembered. We associate precisely this with the role of the prophet – standing up and speaking the truth regardless of the danger of so doing – but it started with Nathan for which we owe him respect as well as gratitude.

***

Huldah makes an appearance in the second book of Kings and although we know much less about her than about other prophets we can discern from the text a significant amount of information.

Huldah is datable to the late seventh century BCE and the context in which she appears is one fraught with profound anxiety about the moral state of the kingdom of Judah. The king, Josiah, had ascended the throne of Judah when he was a boy of eight on the death of his father Amon, but his active governance did not begin until he was eighteen. One of his first actions was to initiate a refurbishment of the Jerusalem Temple, and it was during that work that a discovery was made whose content was to reshape not just the kingdom but Jewish history.

The High Priest of the Temple, Hilkiah, finds a scroll in the Temple which he gives to Shaphan the king's scribe to read to the king.

When Josiah hears its contents he is devastated by it, indicating as it does that the kingdom and all that is in it has fallen far short of the expectations of God. Josiah realises that this must pose a significant existential threat to his rule and his people, unless he acts with dispatch.

His action then is a surprise: instead of giving immediate orders to Temple and palace officials, all of whom would be male, he instead instructs the High Priest and his own most senior courtiers to enquire of the Lord as to what he should do.

Now we might imagine that this was a relatively simple thing for the High Priest to accomplish seeing as he was the most senior religious authority in the land, but this is not what Josiah wants.

To hear the word of the Lord and get divine guidance what they need to do is to consult Huldah the prophetess who lives in Jerusalem. Huldah is married to Shallum, whose father's and grandfather's names are given, though there is no information on Huldah's parentage. That she is known beforehand as one who can deliver the word of God, a key part of the prophet's function, is proved by the fact that it is to her that the delegation is sent as a first port of call and emphasised by the inclusion of the High

Priest in that delegation. The fact that her husband is a royal official, the keeper of the wardrobe, is an interesting detail perhaps suggesting that the king might have encountered Huldah before, but any implication that she is being consulted because of who her husband is gets blown away by the forceful torrent of words Huldah unleashes on the men standing before her and the fact that they express the will of God.[xxiv]

Her oracle is in two parts: the first promises dire destruction for the people's idolatry and apostasy; the second reassures the king that his self-abasement when the scroll was read to him, the tearing of his clothes, guarantees that he will sleep peacefully with his ancestors and will not witness the cataclysm when it comes.

When the officials return to Josiah and relate what Huldah has told them God will do the king asks no questions but immediately acts, initiating a purge of idolaters and idolatrous cults across his country, the most significant reforms for generations.[xxv]

It may be frustrating that we know all too little about the prophetess Huldah as a woman, but the respect she enjoys from the highest in the land, as well as their consulting her rather than her great contemporary Jeremiah, demonstrates that she was honoured and deemed a worthy counsellor of kings and high priests.

Chapter 4

Ahijah, Micaiah and Elijah

Key texts: 1 Kings 14.1-18; 1 Kings 17.1-19.21, 21, 22.1-29; 2 Kings 1.1-2.15
Dates: ca. 10th–9th centuries BCE

Ahijah, like Gad and like Micaiah, is something of a prophetic bit-part player though each has his 'hour upon the stage' and makes the most of it. Ahijah, a resident of Shiloh in the Samarian hills where the pre-Jerusalem Temple Israelite shrine was located, must have been well-known for the first king of the northern kingdom of Israel, Jeroboam 1st, to have advised his wife to go there in disguise and ask the prophet whether their sick son would live.

We are told that Ahijah is blind and that God acts as a kind of magician's assistant telling him that a woman is coming disguised to see him about her son, enabling Ahijah to unmask her, a nasty shock that served only to presage the prophetic denunciation that was to follow.[xxvi]

We know from the great literary prophets who we will investigate later that they were capable of using the most uplifting and elevated language, but this is not what the king's wife gets from Ahijah.

Ahijah assures the queen that her son will die, but then launches a tirade of invective against the king, her husband, and his dynasty, retainers and others in his household, describing them coarsely as destined to be swept away as effluent is sluiced down the street; significantly he also prophesies the exile that awaits the northern kingdom (the Assyrians conquered Israel in 722 BCE and deported its entire population, never to return), the first prophet to do so.[xxvii]

***

Micaiah ben Imlah appears towards the end of the first book of Kings in the context of a joint military operation between the kings of Israel and Judah against their neighbour, the predatory kingdom of Aram. His interjection is set not only against the fact that the king of Israel (Ahab) hates him – 'for he only prophesises bad rather than good for me' – but also that the court prophets of the two kings, a group of sycophants who tell their rulers precisely what they wish to hear whether it is true or not, hate him also.

The story has, unusually for the Hebrew Bible where such moments are rare, a consciously humorous prelude when one of the court prophets is prancing around with iron horns, as a symbol, he tells the kings, of the goring they will administer to the Arameans. Then all the other prophets join in having put on their rose-tinted glasses and tell the kings that God has given them victory.

Micaiah is tipped off about what they have said and advised to echo the words which had been to their masters' liking, but he slaps down the advice saying bluntly, 'I shall only say what the Lord has told me'. Yet when he stands before Ahab he appears to repeat the message of the court prophets. We are momentarily stunned, what happened to 'only saying what God tells him?'

That he is toying with Ahab is made apparent when the king himself tells him to repeat what God has said to him, truthfully, not the other guff which he has been fed. Micaiah replies, simply but terribly, by saying that he had seen the combined army scattered across the hills like sheep. Ahab turns to his fellow king Jehoshaphat and says, 'See? I told you he didn't like me!'[xxviii]

Micaiah, adding the detail that the words he is about to impart are what he heard spoken when he saw God sitting on a throne surrounded by the angelic host, details Ahab's doom and the fact that God is deliberately setting him up as a fall guy by putting false words into the mouths of his so-called prophets. At this point Zedekiah, the court prophet who had worn the horns and who seems quite highly strung, steps forward and hits Micaiah round the face, asking him for the direction that the spirit of God had passed from him to Micaiah. If this is intended as a crushing verbal strike Micaiah bats him away with a put down to which the prophet responds by trying to have him put in prison. Micaiah has the last word, effectively telling the man that his death will prove that he, Micaiah, truly spoke God's word.

It is knockabout stuff, yet that should not disguise the very high stakes for which all the participants are playing nor the courage of the prophet who, in the most highly charged of all highly charged settings, is prepared to say precisely what his interlocutors don't want to hear.

***

Elijah the Tishbite is the first of the prophets to have a major impact not just in the Hebrew Bible but on subsequent Jewish tradition. Elijah is something of a hard, wild man; like the deserts in which he appears to be the most comfortable he is flinty and gritty, his appearance is strange, even alarming and his zeal for his God is towering. Elijah is the nemesis of the King of Israel, Ahab, and especially of his Phoenician wife Jezebel.

We see both sides of Elijah in his first appearance in 1st Kings when he proclaims a drought and a famine to Ahab which lasts for nearly three years, a crude but effective way of demonstrating to a man for whom he mostly feels contempt that it is God who is the one with the power, not him. Elijah then goes and ensures food supplies for a widow and her son, later resurrecting the boy from the dead, an extraordinary act that reinforces his credentials as God's own prophet.[xxix]

The darker side of Elijah's zeal is readily apparent in his great showpiece demonstration of God's power against that of Ba-al. Jezebel, a Ba-al worshipper, has been persecuting other Israelite prophetic groups and this is the time for payback. He goes to the king and demands a public showdown on Mount Carmel.

The Israelites gather to witness, as do some 450 prophets of Ba-al, and Elijah sets the scene for the people telling them that what is to take place will prove once and for all that the God of Israel, not Ba-al, is the God to

24

worship. Elijah demonstrates himself to be a good actor and showman at this event: he has two sacrificial altars set up and invites the prophets of Ba-al to call down fire to consume their bull sacrifice. In spite of strenuous efforts, with a more than comical edge in the biblical telling, the 450 are unsuccessful.

Then it is Elijah's turn and how he relishes it. His altar is full of symbolic power, containing twelve stones for the twelve tribes of Israel, and he then proceeds, as any good magician would, to raise the stakes by saturating the wood on the altar, making the sacrificial act he is about to perform apparently impossible. When he succeeds the Israelite onlookers are amazed, flinging themselves to the ground in an act of humility and penitence and loudly proclaiming their faith in God.

Elijah then commands the crowd to corral the prophets of Ba-al so that he can slaughter them all in a wadi.[xxx]

The Hebrew verb used for this massacre is usually applied to the killing of animals rather than people, perhaps suggesting an aftermath that was redolent of an abattoir.

Even if the numbers in the story have been inflated, Elijah's zealotry for his God is here transformed into bloody fanaticism; his binary world view is as harsh as the desert, and having invoked God's direct intervention he then irrevocably tarnishes it by committing an act of brutal blood-letting that he had not been commanded to perform.

Another outcome – all too predictable we might say – of his massacre of Jezebel's prophets is the queen's vow to wreak bloody retribution on Elijah:[xxxi] brave though he may be Elijah is not foolish, and he flees south to the mountain of Horeb, the mountain of Moses, the mountain of the Ten Commandments, where he is under divine protection.

Elijah is now at a very low ebb: he is in fear of his life, he is alone, and he is resentful when God asks him what he is doing in a mountain cave? 'I'm here,' he says, 'because I have zealously defended your honour against everybody, and now my very life is at risk!' The reassurance that he might be needing is not forthcoming, instead God tells Elijah to stand out on the mountain.

What follows is a lesson that God clearly feels Elijah needs to learn: wind and earthquake and fire pass before his eyes, but God is not in any of them; then, a still small voice, a soft murmuring sound, is heard, and this is the true voice of God, asking the prophet the same question as before. The answer that Elijah gives, though verbally identical lacks the petulance, the neediness, of its first utterance. Here, Elijah simply states the facts – he has done what he has for the glory of God – yet his life is threatened.[xxxii]

It is then that God gives him the reassurance he craves, albeit in a somewhat roundabout way.

'Go home', God tells him, 'the way you came here and as you pass through anoint a new king of Aram, a new king of Israel and someone called Elisha who will succeed you as prophet'.[xxxiii]

Now that may not sound particularly uplifting except for one important factor; all these matters will take time, and if he is to retrace his steps and fulfil important tasks having done so it can only mean that he is safe, that God will protect him. And the first of the three he meets is his successor Elisha, who cannot be a disciple to a dead master!

The next encounter between King Ahab and his nemesis Elijah concerns the vineyard of one Naboth, a place longed for by Ahab but the sale of which Naboth refuses. In one of those typical exercises of absolute power Jezebel sets Naboth up for execution on false charges and, once he has been stoned to death, she gifts the vineyard to her husband.[xxxiv]

His joy at getting what he has long coveted is to be short-lived, however, for God sends Elijah to confront the royal couple and pronounce their doom. This Elijah does almost with relish, telling Ahab that his entire household will be eradicated, and that Jezebel's corpse will be eaten by dogs as if it were mere carrion. The Bible doesn't tell us how Jezebel responded to this pronouncement – though we can probably guess – but it does detail Ahab crumpling, dressing in sackcloth and being penitent. The Bible says that God deferred the destruction of Ahab's dynasty until after his death because of this repentance, but perhaps it hints at the fact that there might just have been an ounce of compassion beneath Elijah's craggy exterior.[xxxv]

Elijah's last days are dominated by an episode where he behaves true to his zealous, cantankerous old self.[xxxvi]

Ahab's successor, Ahaziah, has an accident at home which leaves him seriously injured. His recourse to discover his fate should be Elijah, but he is the son of an idol-worshipper and so sends to the oracle of a pagan god, Ba-al Zevuv, in Ekron one of the five Philistine cities, the others being Ashkelon, Ashdod, Gath and Gaza. Forgetting that God sees everything, Ahaziah is surprised when his envoys return quickly with the news that they bumped into a man on the way; 'What did he look like?' the king asks, 'Covered with hair and wearing a hairy loincloth!' comes the answer. 'That's Elijah!' says the king. 'Yes', reply his envoys, 'and he said you have no hope!'

In the meantime, Elijah has taken up station on a hilltop to await developments. The king misguidedly thinks that if he dresses up the request with a little more authority he may get a better answer.

So he sends a military delegation of an officer and fifty men who are consumed by fire called down by Elijah because the officer is rude to him.

Another delegation follows and is consumed in the same way. The officer leading the third is wiser than the others and takes a supplicatory approach to Elijah, pleading for his life and the life of his men, to which the prophet (reassured by an angel that his life is not in danger) responds positively, going with them to the king and repeating his dire prediction to his face.

This is Elijah's last recorded prophetic act, and it may leave some readers with a bitter taste and a somewhat negative assessment. Why would he act so callously and harshly to men who were not inherently bad but rather doing their duty? Was it just that he was a bad tempered and irritable old man? The answer is revealed in the words of the angel telling Elijah to go with the third military delegation and not to be afraid.

Although the biblical text reveals nothing about Elijah's mental state (why was he sitting on top of a hill?!) the idea that he was fearing for his life makes the action he took a response to that fear and perceived threat, the words of the first two officers hardly suggesting to the prophet that the king's intentions were benign.

The rabbis would probably have exonerated Elijah on the basis of their ruling that 'if someone is out to kill you kill him first' (BT Berakhot 58a, on Exodus 22.1), and we should not be surprised by Elijah's readiness to kill his enemies having read about his massacre of the prophets of Ba-al.

It is the final act of his life, however, which gives him a unique role in Jewish tradition, and which is intimately linked to the beginning of Elisha's prophetic career.

Chapter 5

Elisha

Key texts: 1 Kings 19.19-21; 2 Kings 2.1-9.3; 13.14-21
Date: 9th century BCE

Elisha becomes the acolyte of Elijah quite suddenly. When we are introduced to him he is living with his parents, whom he loves deeply, and working on the family farm. One day Elijah appears and, having already been told that Elisha is his successor, throws his cloak over him.[xxxvii] Elisha's response, without Elijah speaking even a single word, is to kiss his parents farewell and then follow Elijah! As the time draws near for Elijah to die, something which seems to have been widely known, Elisha sticks to his master like glue until they reach the river Jordan to which Elijah has been directed by God. There Elijah removes his aforementioned cloak, strikes the river so that it parts, and the two cross on dry land to the east bank. It is at this point, knowing the end is close that Elijah asks Elisha what he can do for him: 'Give me twice your spirit', comes the answer. 'I will, but only if you see me depart.' Elisha watches until a fiery chariot drawn by fiery horses appears and carries Elijah aloft in the vortex of a whirlwind. As he watches, awed and afraid, Elisha exclaims one of the most enigmatic phrases in the Hebrew Bible: 'My father, my father, Israel's chariots and horsemen.'[xxxviii]

To us this may seem a strange way of saying goodbye but it can make sense. When Elisha calls Elijah *avi*, my father, he expresses the depth of the love and loyalty he feels for the man he succeeds, as well perhaps as his own inadequacy when compared to his master. His talk of chariots and horsemen may express the impact of Elijah's mode and manner of departure on him; or it might be a neat reversal of Stalin's fabled question about the Pope –

How many tanks does the Pope have? – expressing the view that Elijah the prophet was worth more to his people than a brigade of chariots.

Either way this is a powerful and dramatic way of ending Elijah's prophetic role – we know that the old man enjoyed a bit of theatre – and starting Elisha's, but we have to ask why Elisha wanted to be given twice Elijah's spirit.

The easy answer, that he wanted to be twice as effective as his master, suggests an arrogance and self-confidence that I do not think can be correctly attributed to Elisha. In effect, I believe, what he is saying is a sign of his own anxiety about measuring up to his teacher; if he has twice Elijah's spirit he may be half as good, a sentiment shared by many disciples!

The answer to the question of whether he has received it is provided almost immediately afterwards when Elisha strikes the Jordan himself and it parts again to enable him to walk back across the river to the Jericho side.[xxxix] The band of itinerant prophets who had been shadowing Elijah on his final journey and who are watching these events unfold know that by this act Elijah's spirit has indeed passed to Elisha, even if they do not realise that for such a happening Elijah must have left the earth rather than relocating elsewhere by a somewhat flamboyant mode of transport.

The prophetic group come and pledge their loyalty to Elisha, and after they have abortively searched for Elijah Elisha leaves them and begins to walk through the hill country going through the centre of Judah up to Mt Carmel and then back to Samaria. Along the way he acts more like a shaman and healer than a prophet, purifying water and helping the needy to survive; and there is one incident along the way in which he acts like an angry and rather vindictive man, revealing a less than welcome side to his character. In Bethel he is insulted by some of the village children who rather rudely swear at him, twice, 'sod off, baldy!' Impolite maybe, but kids surely are kids? This is not how Elisha sees it though, he curses them in God's name and shortly thereafter two bears come out of the forest and maul no less than forty-two of them![xl]

30

Prophets may be aware of the dignity of their position and the respect due to their authority, but when linked to Elisha's request for a double portion this incident reinforces the sense of the prophet's insecurity in his new role and a concomitant need to be shored up by the respect of others... why else would he lash out in such a horrible way?

Afterwards, Elisha continues in his role as a shaman, first promising a woman whose hospitality he enjoys that she will give birth to a son and then reviving the son after he dies suddenly, possibly of heat stroke.[xli] He also enables Na-aman, a senior military figure in the kingdom of Aram, Israel's powerful and aggressive northern neighbour, to be purified of a serious skin affliction by dipping himself in the Jordan, in so doing making Na-aman a convert to the God of Israel.[xlii]

He raises an axe head that has fallen into a river while a man was cutting down a tree, by putting a branch in the water and making the metal axe head float:[xliii] he also enlists God's help when the king of Aram surrounds the village in which he is staying, and later promises a lifting of the siege of Samaria by the Arameans, providing food for the city's starving inhabitants.[xliv]

It is then that Elisha, like Elijah before him, starts to interfere in royal politics. In Aram, so often Israel's nemesis, he plays a significant part in a royal coup even though he knows that the man who will commit regicide will be a vicious enemy of Israel: he contributes to a coup in Israel that will see an army commander called Jehu rise up against the king of Israel, Joram, killing the king himself, destroying every surviving male of the house of Ahab and, to complete the fulfilment of Elijah's original prophecy to Ahab, having his widow Jezebel thrown to her death from an upstairs window of the royal palace.[xlv]

With these bloody events in which he had played a significant role, apart from a deathbed scene, Elisha disappears from the Hebrew Bible. He is the last of the prophets to act as a shaman, the last to interfere with the royal regimes of his time in such a hands-on and bloody way. The rabbis believed that his prophetic career lasted for sixty years, and if it was indeed a long one it may well have been the case that he was much more of an itinerant healer and miracle worker than a full-blown prophetic figure like those who come later.

It is intriguing that it was Elijah not Elisha who became a major figure in rabbinic literature and from there to a unique role in Jewish mythology. The biblical text suggests that Elijah ascended alive to heaven in his fiery chariot, and from this the rabbis extrapolated that he wandered, and still wanders, the earth waiting to announce the coming of the Messiah. He is heavily disguised at all times, though the especially righteous may recognise him, and all Jews hope to welcome him to their Passover Seder meals when a door is opened and wine provided for him. His biblical story which is awash with blood and fanaticism does not suggest that he would be deemed worthy of such an exalted and fabled future, but we have no text which says he died so the rabbis drew their own conclusions.

Elisha had his brutal side, but his compassion and concern for the disadvantaged seems to have been greater than that of his illustrious master. Yet the Bible tells us he died.

When that time came the king of Israel, Joash, visits the prophet on his death bed, cries over him and utters the same phrase spoken by Elisha when Elijah was taken from him, 'My father, my father, the chariots of Israel and its horsemen'. Perhaps this demonstrates to the ailing Elisha that he has at the end of his career become as great as his master Elijah. His final act from his death bed is to help Joash perform an act of 'sympathetic magic' with a bow and arrows, symbolic of his future victories in battle against the Arameans.[xlvi]

Elisha's grave seems to have become a place of great spiritual importance, almost a portal to heaven in the manner of post-biblical saints, and the final reference to him in second Kings tells of a dead man being thrown into the sepulchre, touching the prophet's bones and being revived from the dead.[xlvii] This seems a fitting ending for someone whose career as a prophet was often concerned with changing people's situation from bad to better, and their state from dead to alive.

MAJOR PROPHETS

Chapter 6

Isaiah

Key texts: 2 Kings 19–20; the Book of Isaiah
Date: 8th century BCE

Isaiah is the first of the Major Prophets in the order they appear in the Hebrew Bible and he was very different from some of his prophetic colleagues. Why? Because he was an aristocrat, possibly even a member of the royal family, and he seems to glide though his prophetic career avoiding the pitfalls and psychodramas of some of his fellow prophets. His first entrance is to be found in second Kings where he is consulted by a delegation of senior courtiers of the reigning monarch Hezekiah after Rabshakeh, the commander of the Assyrian army drawn up outside Jerusalem, has indulged in possibly the first description of what is today called psy-ops (psychological warfare) and threatened the city's and the king's survival.[xlviii]

Isaiah smoothly reassures the king telling him via the delegation that the Assyrians will be unsuccessful, that God will delude the Assyrian king, Sennacherib, that he will return to his own land due to threats to his rule and will there die a violent death.

The next message from the Assyrian commander, which is just as terrifying and portentous as the first, gets a very different reception. Buoyed up by what he has been told by Isaiah, Hezekiah takes Rabshakeh's letter to the Temple and prays fervently to God to punish the Assyrians, not just for the damage to other kingdoms and peoples caused by their rampage through the region, but for their blasphemy in asserting that they were doing the will of God.[xlix]

Isaiah then delivers God's response to Hezekiah's prayer, a towering denunciation of Sennacherib's arrogance and blasphemy and the brutality and destructiveness of his army. He concludes by assuring the king that Jerusalem will not be harmed in any way.[l] Sure enough that night an angel comes and kills 185,000 Assyrian soldiers, Sennacherib retreats to Nineveh, Assyria's capital, and while praying in a temple he is assassinated by two of his sons in a palace coup.[li]

Shortly afterwards, perhaps caused by the strain he has been under, Hezekiah falls gravely ill and Isaiah tells the king that he is going to die.

Hezekiah's response is to turn to the wall of his bedroom and pray to God, asking God to remember the good he has done during his life. The prayer works and Isaiah, still within the palace precincts, is told by God to return to the king's bedside, promise him fifteen extra years and assure him of God's protection. Isaiah acts somewhat shaman-like by asking for a fig poultice to be applied to the king's skin after which he is healed.[lii]

In their final exchange in the book of Kings Isaiah speaks to Hezekiah after a state visit by the king of Babylon during which Hezekiah has shown his guest all his possessions and military capability. The depth of Isaiah's anger with the king for his lack of guile emerges when he delivers another divine pronouncement prophesying that the Babylonians would one day plunder Jerusalem and carry off Hezekiah's descendants to be eunuchs in the Babylonian court. This is a chilling message, even though it is catastrophe postponed, but Hezekiah accepts it without demurral.[liii]

**

There are sixty-six chapters in the Book of Isaiah and a raft of scholarly suggestions about who wrote which parts. The consensus is that chapters 1 to 39 were written by the actual Isaiah, dating from the eighth century BCE, chapters 40 to 66 by a second person (Second Isaiah) living in Babylon, or a second and third individual (Second and Third Isaiah) living in Jerusalem, dated after the return from exile in Babylon when Palestine was under Persian rule in the late sixth/early fifth centuries BCE.

Some of the most glorious material in the Book of Isaiah is found in the last twenty-seven chapters, influential in both Jewish and Christian traditions, but I shall focus initially on the first thirty-nine chapters of the Isaiah who prophesied in the eighth and early seventh century BCE during the reigns of four kings of Judah – Uzziah, Jotham, Ahaz and Hezekiah. This was a period during which the kingdom came under the cosh wielded by the Assyrians who were flexing their muscles and who posed a serious existential threat.

Isaiah, an easy mover between royal, temple and popular circles spared no one in his prophetic oracles. His career began one day in the Temple when he had a vision of God sitting on a throne surrounded by seraphs who proclaimed: 'Holy, holy, holy is the commander of the hosts of heaven, his glorious presence fills the entire earth.' Isaiah's response to this vision is to fear for his life.

Isaiah has the ability to hear what is being said by the angels around the divine throne but it is only after one of those angels has touched his lips with a coal taken from the Temple altar and 'purified' him that he can hear God's voice. And what does he hear: 'Who shall we send? Who will go for us?'

Now it is common, as we shall see, for those asked by God to become prophets to hedge a little before giving an affirmative answer – no one says 'no' and gets away with it! But Isaiah almost falls over himself in his eagerness to serve God as he instantly responds to God's questions: 'Hear am I, send me!' He doesn't ask what the mission is in advance of accepting it and the answer he receives is not especially encouraging. Essentially God tells him in advance that no one who hears him will listen to what he has to say; if Isaiah responds to this built-in failure clause the Bible doesn't share this detail with us, but from the oracles and pronouncements that follow he just gets on with the job.[liv]

Like all the truly significant prophets Isaiah is motivated by a loathing of the way the poor and disadvantaged are treated by the rich and privileged. He proclaims loudly that this is contrary to the will of God and to the laws of the covenant relationship between God and Israel. And the inevitable outcome of disobeying the laws of the covenant is the breaking of that covenant and an ending of the lovingkindness and protection of God.

Isaiah, like other prophets before and after him, did not hold back from delivering a disturbing message and sometimes, as can happen with all public speakers, he got the bit between his teeth and let rip. He abhorred the abuse of privilege, the greed of the haves to have more, the corruption of justice and other structures by which a society maintains its internal cohesion.

His principal target, shared with other prophets, was the cult of temple sacrifice and the abuse thereof. When you have a system in place which enables you to pay for an animal to be sacrificed as an expiation of wrongdoing without yourself having to do anything else, then abuse is inevitable. Isaiah fought hard to get the message through to the people that good behaviour in the Temple and good behaviour outside had to be synonymous, and if right actions within were counter-balanced by bad behaviour without then the former was cancelled out by the latter.[lv]

It might be expected that this approach would have made Isaiah unpopular with the people and the priests, but from the security offered by his status he appears to have had no trouble from either regardless of his strictures and condemnations.

He lays in to the women of Jerusalem who walk in the city with 'roving eyes and mincing gait', itemising every single piece of clothing and jewellery that they will lose and the degradation they will suffer when their menfolk are killed and they have none to protect them.[lvi] It is hard to read such language in the twenty-first century without wondering whether this isn't partly an example of classic misogyny rather than a denunciation of excess and immorality, though using modern criteria and cultural norms to judge another period, let alone one as far back as the eighth century BCE, is never particularly helpful.

Either way this is an uncomfortable side to Isaiah, but there is much more against which he inveighs.

A popular target for many prophets including Isaiah were the nations around their own: why should this be the case when Isaiah felt there was so much to rail against in his own country? The answer partly lies in the fact that Judah and Israel, or 'the Israelites' before the kingdoms existed, had 'history' with many of these countries, making the diatribes a partial payback for old wrongs and enmities. It may also be the case that as idolatrous nations, perhaps as such meriting less divine concern, they were an easy target for an angry prophet to get his own audience onside for prophecies closer to home and the early chapters of the book suggest that Isaiah was a fine orator possessing many of the tricks that speakers across the ages have used to manipulate their listeners.

How much impact did these particular prophecies have on the nations against which they were directed? As this was a time when material that was communicated from one place to another took as long to reach its destination as the person bearing it, the sort of immediacy which we understand was not possible.

In addition, with no journalists only court historians, the words carried by those who had heard the original prophetic utterance would not, on arrival days or weeks later, possess quite the same impact they did when first spoken. In any case, if targets were great nations like Egypt, it is unlikely that they cared any more than the United States cares when 'Death to America' is chanted at the end of Friday prayers in Teheran.

The Book of Isaiah is a regular source for prophetic readings in Jewish worship following the reading of the Torah, and this may be attributed not only to the messages contained therein but also to the fine language in which the messages are couched. This use of words is apparent in all the utterances of the prophet, for good and bad.

An example of the latter can be found in the Babylon pronouncement[lvii] where Isaiah almost relishes the doom he speaks:

Then like gazelles that are chased and like sheep that no man gathers, each man shall turn back to his people, they shall flee everyone to his land. All who remain shall be pierced through, all who are caught shall fall by the sword. And their babies shall be dashed to pieces in their sight, their homes shall be plundered and their wives shall be raped.[lviii]

This is grim reading to be sure, but in its context probably buoyed the listeners with an expression of vengeance from *God* for the suffering *they* had endured.[lix] However fine Isaiah's choice of imagery may be, it is worth remembering that those who use such chillingly vivid language probably do so because their own people have endured precisely the same things.

In the pronouncement against Egypt[lx] Isaiah starts as he has with previous denunciations; God is coming to smite Egypt riding on a cloud, there will be a civil war, despair everywhere, and a harsh ruler will govern them with ruthlessness. They may look to salvation from the Nile but it too will fail them, and all those who depend upon it; the wisest of Pharaoh's advisers will have nothing constructive to offer and Egypt is described as being as incapacitated as a vomiting drunkard.

But the diatribe then takes a sudden twist for it talks of a time to come when there will not just be peace between Assyria and Egypt but they will partner with Israel and all will worship the God of Israel.[lxi]

Isaiah may indulge in the rhetoric of his time but he is also aware that the God who speaks to him has positive outcomes in mind for those he criticizes after a period of punishment has purified them, and this applies to Judah and Israel as much as to their neighbours. We do not know whether the positives stuck in Isaiah's craw as hard as the denunciations that flowed from it, but as a prophet he was there to speak the words God had given him regardless of his own opinions.

So was speaking, denouncing, terrifying and condemning all that Isaiah did?

We have some answers to that question because 2 Kings has revealed him as a court intimate and adviser to the king. But was there anything else? The answer is yes, for Isaiah performed a number of symbolic acts designed to affect and influence. In view of his oracle concerning the remnant of Israel that would remain after God had purified them Isaiah named one of his sons *She-ar Yashuv*, 'a remnant shall remain'; another was called, somewhat less clearly *Maher-Shalal Hash Baz*, 'pillage hastens, looting speeds', indicating that a disaster is about to befall the cities of Damascus and Samaria at the hands of the Assyrians.[lxii]

Later, in the year that the Assyrians besieged Ashdod (711), God instructed Isaiah to remove his clothes and his sandals and walk around naked and bare-foot as a sign of the fate awaiting Egypt and Ethiopia.[lxiii] However effective or otherwise Isaiah's words may have been there can be little doubt that an elderly man walking the streets like some itinerant *sadhu*, let alone an elderly man who was an esteemed prophet and intimate of the king, would have circulated like wildfire and the assumption must have been that whatever it portended was really bad.

Isaiah may have been God's mouthpiece but he was also human and, as with all humans, he had his frailties and one in particular was his deep dislike for a senior royal official called Shebna.

It is said of Her Majesty Queen Elizabeth II that one of the things she cannot abide is pomposity and 'airs and graces', and it may well be that Isaiah had a similar contempt for those who acted way above their station. The focus for his ire, Shebna, the major domo of the Palace, was the king's steward. We can only imagine the state of his relationship with Isaiah, himself possibly a member of the royal family, and a man who stood up for the poor and weak and held those who should know better to account. We know nothing specific of their relationship so cannot say for sure whether the outburst[lxiv] in chapter 22 came after years of enmity or was an explosion of anger at Shebna's plans to build himself a mausoleum in the Kidron valley opposite Jerusalem, a project that Isaiah found vainglorious at the very least.

The Hebrew text contains puns, repetitions and, if read with feeling, comes over as staccato and incredibly aggressive. The diatribe assumed greater status when in 1870 a tomb was discovered by archaeologists which, though badly damaged, had an inscription above its entrance which stated:

41

This is ... [the tomb of Shebna] ...iah, the royal steward. There is no silver or gold here, only ... [his bones] ... and the bones of his maidservant with him. Cursed be the man who opens this.

The fact that the name is in brackets means that there was a gap in the inscription, but the ending of the name, and the identification 'royal steward' made the reconstruction quite confident. In addition, the tomb was found where the Bible indicated it would be;[lxv] but the discovery, if indeed that of the tomb of Shebna, rather undermines Isaiah's pronouncement that the grave would never be used because remains were found therein presumably belonging to the royal steward.

What this oracle tells us about Isaiah that we would not otherwise have known is that he was not a man whose vision was restricted to prophetic specifics, but rather that he was a flesh and blood human being with likes and dislikes, passions and rages. To me it makes him and the text that bears his name even more special, for it shows the prophet's frailty as well as his strength.

What many of us who study the Bible associate with the Book of Isaiah are some of the most important texts in Judaeo-Christian civilisation and some of the most sublime language in the entire Hebrew Bible.

From his vision of a messianic future when *'a shoot from the stock of Jesse will be imbued with God's spirit, will judge the poor with equity and girdle his loins with justice, and when the order of the natural world will be overturned';*[lxvi] to the moment when *'the people who walked in darkness have seen a great light, and those living in a place of darkness have seen daylight dawn';* [lxvii] to the day when *'the eyes of the blind shall be opened and the ears of the deaf unstopped; then the lame shall leap like a deer and the tongue of the speechless sing for joy.'*[lxviii] Mention Isaiah to anyone familiar with the Bible and it is these verses which will most readily spring to mind.

For Christians one text in Isaiah counts above all others: *'A young woman is pregnant and will bear a son and she will name him Immanuel.'*[lxix] And for

Progressive Jews, repeated prominently in the liturgy it is the vision of reconciliation that comes near the start of the book:

> In the days to come, the mountain of the Lord's house shall stand firm above the mountains and tower above the hills; and all the nations shall gaze on it with joy. And the many peoples shall go and say 'Come, let us go up to the Mount of the Lord, to the House of the God of Jacob; that He may instruct us in His ways and that we may walk in His paths'. For instruction shall come forth from Zion, and the word of God from Jerusalem. [lxx]

Glorious quotes do not, however, end with Isaiah chapter 39, indeed chapters 40 to 66 contain material that has also been extremely influential in the Judaeo-Christian biblical tradition. As noted earlier, there are differing theories about the authorship of these chapters though not so much about their date.

This section of Isaiah is almost universally deemed to have been post-exilic, written after the Babylonian exile of the Jews of Judah in the sixth century BCE was ended by the Persian conquest of the Babylonian empire. The Persians, ruled by Cyrus, had a policy of returning former exiles to the land of their birth and allowing them some autonomy. Wisely they deemed this a better way of ensuring loyalty and peace than might be the case with iron-fisted rule.

The return, of which we read in the books of Ezra and Nehemiah, was a truly blessed moment and the prophetic response of Second Isaiah was to laud Cyrus for his beneficence and see him as the instrument of God.

This concept is not original to Second Isaiah, Jeremiah describes the Babylonian king Nebuchadnezzar as the instrument of God's punishment,[lxxi] but here the instrument is one of benignity and mercy; the reference to Cyrus in Isaiah 44[lxxii] calls him *'God's shepherd, who fulfils what God desires'*, and lauds him for his permission to allow the Temple in Jerusalem to be built. The following chapter, replete with the soaring, lyrical language that is Second Isaiah's hallmark, goes even further describing God as being actively involved in Cyrus' triumphs, the ultimate purpose of them all being the restoration of Zion.[lxxiii]

So many texts in the opening ten chapters attributed to Second Isaiah are possessed of such beauty, and have become so widely known, that it is a shock to find him succumbing to the sort of bitter invective that characterises other prophets; but in chapter 47 he lays into Babylon, a reminder that behind the optimism and hope of preceding chapters lies the resentful fury of a wronged and exiled people.[lxxiv] This is, though, but an interlude in the elevated nature of these chapters and the real sense they convey of wrongs purged and sins forgiven, of a relationship between God and the people of Israel back on track.

Chapter 53 stands out from the chapters in this section of Isaiah because it has been for millennia a key 'Old Testament' text deemed to foretell the coming of Jesus, and to describe aspects of his life. Extracts appear in Handel's great oratorio *Messiah*, together with several other selected verses: the fact that this is not the way this chapter has been interpreted by Jewish scholars has often throughout history been interpreted not as another point of view but a calculated, insulting rejection, making it a battleground that cannot have been its author's intention.

The remaining twelve chapters, 55 to 66, are deemed by some to be the work of a third hand because of certain stylistic differences from previous ones. Suffice it to say that regardless of which is correct these chapters also contain exalted and exalting language, as well as good prophetic bite, not least in chapter 58, the *haftarah* for the morning of Yom Kippur, which reminds readers that outward form observance is not what God requires but rather right thought and motivation, and the section itself also hints at a messianic future time when all will be unified in their worship of the one true God. Whatever scholarly arguments there may be about the origins of the book that bears Isaiah's name it is beyond dispute that its contents have had an unrivalled impact on Judaism and Christianity and is beloved in both traditions.

Chapter 7

Jeremiah

Key texts: the Book of Jeremiah
Dates: 7th–6th century BCE

Jeremiah is arguably the greatest of all the prophets. It is also true that the eponymous book contains more biographical detail than may be found in other prophetic books as well as descriptions of the challenges and danger his role brought him and, most particularly, what being a prophet did to his inner and outer wellbeing.

The book of Jeremiah opens with a brief biography: Jeremiah was born into a priestly family in Anatot, a village southwest of Jerusalem, and his prophetic career spanned forty years, starting in the thirteenth year of the reign of King Josiah (627 BCE) and ending in the eleventh year of Judah's last king, Zedekiah (586 BCE).

What follows is God's call to Jeremiah to be a prophet, and Jeremiah's response. I have already remarked that reluctance to take on the mantle of prophecy was not uncommon, but the starkness of Jeremiah's call is unique.

God's word comes to Jeremiah not with an invitation to become a prophet but an unarguable proposition: '*Before you were in the womb I selected you to be my prophet, before you were born I marked you out as special*', the dye has been cast for quite some time.[lxxv]

Jeremiah responds with a plea similar to that of Moses at the Burning Bush. 'I don't know how to speak in public,' he says, and, 'I'm just a boy'. God does not even respond to the first statement and dismisses the second telling

45

Jeremiah that he is to go where God sends him and say what God tells him to say. And God adds, (in response to an unspoken but likely inner thought, 'I'm scared to do this'), 'have no fear for I will be with you to keep you safe'.[lxxvi]

And then God does something to Jeremiah that none of the other prophets experience, God touches the prophet's mouth, a concrete sign that it is God's words that he will speak.[lxxvii]

This relatively short narrative over, the oracles start pouring out of Jeremiah and his angry diatribes contain many of the complaints found in Isaiah and subsequent prophetic books.

He despises the people's lack of genuine faith and commitment to God, he speaks of a rupture between God and the people of Israel in the terms of a divorce between a man and a woman: but it is also clear from the early chapters of the book onwards that Jeremiah has his eye on the bigger picture. Even more than Isaiah, Jeremiah knows that events in surrounding countries will impact more and more on the kingdom of Judah and it is this awareness which inspires him to make the hugely significant identification of the approaching nemesis with the way the people of Judah behave. There is the possibility of a reprieve but it is remote and dependant on a change of heart and deed by the people.

Other prophets pronounce doom to their people without any apparent personal impact, but that is not the case with Jeremiah. He is not a remote bystander and the cataclysm that is drawing nearer pierces his heart. He expresses his pain and anguish in a unique way:[lxxviii]

> *Oh my suffering, my suffering!*
> *How I writhe!*
> *Oh, the walls of my heart!*
> *My heart moans within me,*
> *I cannot be silent;*
> *For I hear the blare of horns,*
> *Alarms of war.*

This reads to us like a severe panic attack, but worse is to come.

In addition to the stress caused by the message he has to deliver, Jeremiah is also required to contend with other prophets, probably those associated with the Temple or the royal court, whose message is the opposite of his own and who pose a threat to him. But rather than run, Jeremiah stands firm, ridicules these false prophets, and speaks with added fire of the doom that awaits, *'from an ancient kingdom whose language you do not know'.*[lxxix]

These early clashes are, however, a portent of even harder times.

Chapter 7 brings the start of a sermon that Jeremiah gives, at God's instruction, at the very entrance to the Temple in Jerusalem, the very place that gives the Judahites of whom he despairs such false hope and courage.

'Get your act together', Jeremiah shouts at those passing him by, 'and stop doing all those things which drive God to distraction! Don't think you can go around repeating "The Temple of the Lord" three times and all will be well, for it is empty and will achieve nothing. Do you honestly believe that you can do whatever you like, including sacrificing to idols, and then come to God's house and expect to be forgiven and protected?'[lxxx]

This is the start of a long and devastating diatribe during which God says to Jeremiah that he must not plead for mercy on the people's behalf because they are beyond mercy. The only satisfactory path is for them to be punished to such an extent that their lives and their land will be ruined. The language that Jeremiah uses is graphic, terrifying and relentless, and includes such details as the bones of kings and priests and senior officers being exhumed and thrown on the ground as carrion, never to be reburied.[lxxxi]

And yet, he is not an automaton: he is a living, feeling, conflicted man. He may be delivering the word of God, he may have accepted the nature of his relationship with his God, he may know that there is no escape from it, but he is not afraid to express the anguish that it causes him.

Jeremiah may denounce like other prophets, he may intercede on Israel's behalf like other prophets, but what raises him above them all is the insight he gives us into his inner life and the devastating impact on it of being a prophet.

Within this major address we find Jeremiah sick at heart, grief stricken at the fate of his people, saying: [lxxxii]

> *Because my people is shattered I am shattered;*
> *I am dejected, seized by desolation.*

And there will be more, much more, in this vein.

But the main burden of the sermon is the looming exile when the people will be transported to a foreign land by a relentless enemy which we cannot but conclude is doing God's will.

Some of the imagery that Jeremiah uses is immensely powerful and threatening:[lxxxiii]

> *For death has climbed through our windows,*
> *Has entered our fortresses,*
> *To cut off babes from the street,*
> *Young men from the squares.*
> *Speak thus – says the Lord:*
> *The carcasses of men shall lie*
> *Like dung upon the fields*
> *Like sheaves behind the reaper,*
> *With none to pick them up.*

But there are also positive, even didactic, interpolations:[lxxxiv]

> *Let not the wise man glory in his wisdom;*
> *Let not the strong man glory in his strength;*
> *Let not the rich man glory in his riches.*
> *But only in this should one glory:*
> *In his earnest devotion to Me.*

As might be expected, the words that Jeremiah utters against his people and every aspect of the life of his nation gain him the attention of the authorities at a national and local level, but an early threat against his life from the people of Anatot, revealed to him by God, is thwarted by God who promises the prophet that it is his enemies who will be destroyed.[lxxxv]

As the prophecies multiply, as their scope and their all-consuming dread multiplies, so too do the prophet's enemies.

The interests most threatened are those of the Temple priesthood and the royal court and its associates, including its court prophets. This is also what raises Jeremiah to a unique height: he is at loggerheads, not just with the people who have betrayed their God, he is at loggerheads with everyone monarch and priest included.

The court prophets offer the people a message and a vision that is the opposite of Jeremiah's:[lxxxvi] 'All is well, trust in God and the Temple to protect us all,' and, by implication, 'Don't listen to Jeremiah all of whose words are false.' For those in secular authority Jeremiah is bad for morale, his words weakening popular resolve and the societal cohesion on which they depend. Inevitably there will be a serious clash between Jeremiah and his opponents, it is not a question of whether, simply when.

Jeremiah's response to the official prophets is to threaten them, in God's name, with death by the very sword and famine they have denounced him for prophesying and then to continue in the same vein, even though he intersperses it with the agony and the cost inflicted upon him: [lxxxvii]

> *Woe is me, my mother, that you ever bore me –*
> *A man of conflict and strife with all the land!*
> *I have not lent,*
> *And I have not borrowed;*
> *Yet everyone curses me.*[lxxxviii]

The second part of this cry for justice suggests that not only are Jeremiah's prophecies being undermined but also his moral character, presumably to imply that in addition to his traitorous, even blasphemous, words he is no better than the people he denounces.

Yet even now Jeremiah receives further blows from his God as again he is used to make a point to his people. 'You cannot marry or have children here, because a terrible fate awaits the people of this land,' God tells him.[lxxxix] Although it seems clear from the text that God seeks only to save Jeremiah from the fate that will befall other husbands and fathers, which the prophet accepts without argument, the effect of this diktat is to remind him just how lonely he is and will continue to be as the battle for the soul of Judah intensifies.

When Jeremiah hears of another plot against him he turns to God and reminds him how loyal he has been to his prophetic charge, and then asks for God to kill his enemies and their families in the most horrific way possible.[xc] Those who would laud Jeremiah may find this a less than edifying request, but it is wholly in keeping with his humanity and human frailty that Jeremiah, already angered by the threats he faces, and afraid, should wish to see that with which they threaten him inflicted upon them.

After another quite theatrical event at the Valley of Hinnom, when Jeremiah takes an earthen vessel and smashes it before the eyes of his audience as a symbol of Jerusalem's fate, Jeremiah repairs to the Temple court and repeats the message. This act crosses a line for a very senior priest, Pashhur, who, having heard Jeremiah's utterance, has him flogged and either imprisoned or put in the stocks overnight.[xci] [The text may be interpreted either way.] If he had thought Jeremiah would show contrition and a change of heart he is mistaken. As soon as he is released from his humiliation he repeats the essence of his message and adds for good measure that Pashhur and his family will be taken into exile never to return to their native land.[xcii]

However, it is precisely at this point that Jeremiah reaches an inner crisis; the stress of his role, and his own deep depression – for it cannot be anything else – conspiring within him not to plead but to rage against God with words that wrench and twist the heartstrings:

You enticed me O Lord, and I was enticed;
You overpowered me and You prevailed.
I have become a constant laughing-stock,
Everyone jeers at me...
For the word of the Lord causes me
Constant disgrace and contempt...
Accursed be the day
That I was born!
Let not the day be blessed
When my mother bore me!
Accursed be the man
Who brought my father the news
And said 'a boy
Is born to you,'
And gave him such joy![xciii]

This is heart-breaking language, and it is shocking too, for the Hebrew used in the opening verse is of seduction and then rape, an image of stealth leading to violence which is hard to understand in the context of a relationship between God and a prophet; why does God need to 'seduce', why does God need to 'rape'? Part of the answer lies in the nature of the prophetic role – being doomed from the start to be set at odds with the people from which he comes, not just nationally but locally, where he is best known.

We know that Jeremiah never set out to be a prophet, that it was God who had designated him while he was still in the womb (another strange image, unique to Jeremiah and suggesting an invasion by God of Jeremiah's mother).

Perhaps what is surprising is that he doesn't struggle harder against his destiny when it is first spelled out to him but, on the other hand, until he reaches this point in his prophetic career with the stakes rising higher and higher, he cannot have imagined the appalling impact it would have on him.

The fact that he veers between despair and faith in God merely expresses his profound inner turmoil, a depression so profound that rising above it must have been exhausting. It cannot be accidental that he concludes his cry of despair with words that directly echo the language of his call to be a prophet:

> *Because he did not kill me before birth*
> *So that my mother might be my grave,*
> *And her womb big with me for all time.*
> *Why did I ever issue from the womb,*
> *To see misery and woe,*
> *To spend all my days in shame!*[xciv]

Immediately after this cry the stakes are raised again: King Zedekiah sends a high powered delegation asking for an oracle of reassurance from God about the Babylonians and their king, Nebuchadnezzar, who are besieging the city.[xcv] This is close to being an actual audience with the king as Jeremiah's words will be reported verbatim to the king by his closest advisers, and Jeremiah gives his response with both barrels. All is lost, God's face is set against Jerusalem, it will be destroyed by the Babylonians, and the king, his courtiers and his people will be struck down by the sword.[xcvi]

This can hardly have made Jeremiah popular but undaunted he gives more disturbing messages to the king, standing at the gates of the royal palace to reinforce the message of its destruction. From attacking the king the prophet turns his attention to the 'false' prophets, against whom he feels understandable animus: they are to blame for the land's godlessness, they will drink a bitter draft, they are charlatans not sent by God.[xcvii]

To have seriously offended the three major leadership groups in the country brings inevitable troubles and they are not long in manifesting themselves. Having prophesied the destruction of almost all the ancient kingdoms, including his own, at the hands of the Babylonians, encouraging them not just to drink from the cup of woe but to become drunk and then vomit,[xcviii] Jeremiah presents himself at the court of the new king of Judah, Jehoiakim (608–597 BCE) in the hope that a new man on the throne may engender a change of heart among the people. Yet the impact of Jeremiah's threats and doom is to cause a near riot resulting in a proposal from the priests and prophets to execute him! 'Go ahead,' says Jeremiah, 'if you want innocent blood on your hands; I've only done what God required me to do.' And the people and court officials save him.[xcix]

These were fevered times and another prophet, only mentioned briefly, Uriah ben Shemaiah, is hunted down by the king's soldiers, extracted from Egypt to which he had fled, and returned to Jerusalem where he is summarily killed and thrown into a pauper's grave.[c] Jeremiah escapes a similar fate on more than one occasion and after this most recent threat he is taken under the protection of a revered elder, Ahikam ben Shaphan. If we were to think that this would encourage Jeremiah to lie low for a while we would be mistaken.

Now he goes to a level he has never been before: donning a yoke with straps Jeremiah delivers a message which designates Nebuchadnezzar as God's servant, to whom all the surrounding nations shall be subjugated and bear the yoke if they refuse to bow the knee; those who make peace with the Babylonians, however, will be saved.

With this oracle Jeremiah leaves behind the idea of the Babylonians as looming punishment for popular transgression and enunciates a message of co-operation which is all too easily construed as proposing collaboration with the enemy.[ci]

[One of the challenges of this section of Jeremiah is working out who the kings referred to are, especially as some names are differently written and others seem to have only reigned for the blink of an eye. Yehoyakim reigned from 609 to 598 BCE and died in Jerusalem; Yehoyachin, also called Yeconiah and Coniah, reigned for three months in 597BCE before being deported to Babylon; Zedekiah reigned from 597 to 586 before being blinded and taken into exile.]

There follow two exiles: the first in 597 BCE takes away King Yeconiah and his queen, all the senior officials of the kingdom and the leading artisans, leaving a new king, Zedekiah in place; the second in 586 BCE involves further deportations and, even more importantly, the destruction of the Temple and large parts of the city of Jerusalem.

This period, with changes of kings and a growing threat is one of enormous turmoil, and Jeremiah is at its heart. The oracles continue, but the tone changes, and whereas before all was darkness without relief now the message softens, not to reverse the coming destruction and exile but to talk about the remnant who will survive and who will one day return to their land.[cii] Nevertheless, Jeremiah is seen as a thorn in the side of the establishment, an appeaser, and a demoraliser of his people. What follows is similar to previous incidents, but with a sharper edge.

Another clash takes place in the Temple between the prophet and a rival, Hananiah ben Azzur.[ciii] The latter counters Jeremiah with a message purportedly from God announcing that the yoke of the king of Babylon will be broken and everything taken away by Nebuchadnezzar will be restored. Jeremiah's response is aggressive; he unleashes a sarcastic assault on the false prophet, ridiculing him and reminding him of the criteria by which a true prophet may be ascertained. Hananiah, however, is not cowed.

Perhaps he senses that Jeremiah is not quite as strong as he was; he strides towards Jeremiah, removes the yoke from his shoulders, smashes it to the ground and then reasserts his previous message. Jeremiah's response is to storm off but he returns shortly afterwards and denounces Hananiah as a false prophet, telling him that the wooden yoke he smashed will be replaced by one of iron and he will die within a year. Both these predictions are realised.

In spite of the easing of his oracles, the battle between God and his prophet and King Zedekiah and his court reaches a climax when an appeal to the king by his courtiers and officers to execute Jeremiah for treason is accepted.[civ] Jeremiah, who on a previous occasion had to go into hiding for fear of the wrath of Zedekiah's predecessor and communicated God's word via his secretary Barukh ben Neriah, is arrested and thrown into a pit full of mud where he would probably have died had he not been freed by the king after an entreaty from one of his eunuchs, an Ethiopian called Eved Melekh.[cv] Jeremiah is freed from the pit but kept under house arrest until the

Babylonians capture the city when he is released on the command of Nebuchadnezzar himself and allowed to stay with Gedaliah, a member of a prominent family permitted to remain in Judah who had been appointed governor.[cvi]

Jeremiah's story, however, does not end there. In the aftermath of the defeat by the Babylonians and the exile of key parts of the population, anarchy reigns, and there is civil conflict during the course of which Gedaliah is murdered. A group of surviving Judeans, anxious for their future, come to Jeremiah and request that he asks God what they should do: God advises they should stay put and receive his mercy, and above all that they should not relocate to Egypt, for a terrible fate awaits that country and if they go they will be caught up in it.[cvii]

This is a very clear message but the group ignores it, even questioning whether it has come from God at all, and they then leave for Egypt taking Jeremiah and Barukh with them. The measure of this remarkable man may be seen in what follows: after the loss of Gedaliah, followed by his forced removal to Egypt, a move utterly opposed by God, Jeremiah continues to prophesy to the Judahite remnant.

His last series of oracles are mainly directed at other nations, commencing with Egypt but ending with Babylon which, in spite of the fact that its king and his army were earlier designated as agents of the divine will, shall also be destroyed and left desolate as a punishment for its murderous rampage through the ancient Middle East.[cviii]

Jeremiah's final act is to send a scroll containing his Babylonian oracle to be thrown into the Euphrates river as a symbol that the country would sink and never rise again. And that is that – 'Thus far the words of Jeremiah' says the Bible.[cix]

Why, then does Jeremiah deserve the accolades I awarded him at the start of the chapter? Was he not merely another 'turbulent' prophet? Did he not follow a pattern similar to many other prophets, take risks like them, make enemies like them, suffer because of what they were?

There are indeed many similarities between Jeremiah and other prophets, but his concerns had a much broader perspective, not just looking at failings in Judahite society but concerned with matters of *realpolitik*, of the place of his own country in a broader context, and of the need to get these relations right. In addition, his courage and the views he expressed brought him into some humiliating and extremely dangerous situations where escaping with his life was not a given.

And that is not all: we know more about the inner workings of his mind than any other prophet, and we can read his descriptions of the depression that at times threatened to consume him. Jeremiah also had the opportunity to witness the first deportations from Judah, and to consider very carefully what might be the implications for his fellow citizens, the impact of losing everything held dear, everything familiar.

This is where Jeremiah cements his place as *primus inter pares* in the prophetic pantheon. His act of purchasing a plot of land in Anatot may have been a tangible demonstration of his faith in his land and its ultimate survival,[cx] but it was a letter that Jeremiah sent to the first wave of Judahite exiles to Babylon that marked a quantum shift, a game changer.

This letter, sent by Jeremiah to the exiles by the hand of royal emissaries had an important message for its recipients. Had this letter not been sent it is probable that the Judahite exiles of both waves would have suffered the same fate as their co-religionists of the northern kingdom, deported by the Assyrians in 722 BCE never to return.[cxi]

The letter to the entire exile community told them to build houses, plant gardens, eat their fruit and enjoy them. It told them to marry and have children, and then marry off those children so they would also procreate. 'Grow there,' said Jeremiah, 'don't hide away; and above all, pray for the city you live in, and pray to God on its behalf because its wellbeing will also be yours.'[cxii]

All this in a mere six verses! But what they say is in no way commensurate with the number of words in which they say it! Jeremiah is telling the exiles, who on arrival sat down and wept by the rivers of Babylon as they remembered Zion, not to live their lives in anticipation of immediate return but rather to put down roots and do all the things that settled people do. And what is significant is that none of these things are instantaneous, they take time, and not days or weeks but years. Later in the same letter he promises a return from exile to their ancestral land, and a return to divine favour.[cxiii] But just before this Jeremiah has told the exiles to pray to God for the city in which they reside.

It sounds innocuous but in effect it is telling them to establish the regular worship of God in their new home, a ground-breaking directive which at a stroke changes the conceptualisation of God as the God of Israel who can only be effectively worshipped in one place to a universal God who may be worshipped anywhere.

In this way Jeremiah subtly imparts the information that even though the exiles had been forcibly removed from their own land their God had not abandoned them but rather was with them, and thus did Jeremiah help them to avoid despair.

This is the point in the Hebrew Bible, and the history of the Jewish people, when, I believe, we can talk correctly in terms of the beginning of Judaism as distinct from Israelite religion. Once the God of Israel, who is One, becomes the universal God everything changes. This is the ultimate expression of Jeremiah's vision, his wisdom, and his zeal for his God. He saved a righteous remnant, and not just to survive for survival's sake but to survive as the prototype for a new people, the Jewish people, and its universal religion Judaism.

Many of the structures that we associate with Judaism were constructed much later but Jeremiah's letter marks the foundation stone and, in view of everything that stems from it, is entitled to be called one of the most important letters in human history.

So is that it? What happened to Jeremiah? Did he get back to Judah to live on the plot of land we know he bought for this purpose? There is no definitive information in the book that bears his name, but there is a tradition preserved in a rabbinic text called Midrash Aggadah which purports to describe his fate.

Jesus may have been the first to enunciate, 'prophets are not without honour, except in their own town'[cxiv] but if anybody epitomised this truth it was Jeremiah. According to the Midrash, the Jews of Egypt enraged, one must assume by his prophecies, stoned him to death and abandoned his body. The Egyptians, however, buried him because they loved him. Why? Because he had successfully prayed on their behalf that crocodiles would disappear from the Nile and cease to ravage the countryside around it.[cxv]

If there is any truth in this legend it suggests that, as in life, Jeremiah was misunderstood by his own people but respected by those who might be deemed his enemies. A sad end indeed, but a great life.

Postscript: Jewish tradition credits Jeremiah with the authorship of Lamentations, a stark and powerful book of only four chapters responding lyrically and viscerally to the destruction of Jerusalem. Modern scholarship tends to be more equivocal, but it is easy to think that Jeremiah may have been the author of Lamentations because the language seems to speak from his very soul.

Chapter 8

Ezekiel

Key texts: The book of Ezekiel
Date: 6th century BCE

Ezekiel, I once heard it said, was 'one weird dude'! The reasons for this unlikely but not wholly inappropriate description will soon become apparent, but Ezekiel's biography is essential before considering his prophetic career.

Very helpfully for us Ezekiel dates his first Babylonian visions to the fifth of the month of Tammuz 593 BCE. This means that Ezekiel who was from a priestly family, something he shared with his contemporary Jeremiah, was part of the first Babylonian deportation from Judah in 597 BCE. The experience of being among the first to be exiled must have had a significant impact upon him and we know that those forced to move to a land of which they know nothing find it very hard to settle, very hard to let go of the place from which they have come. We cannot know for sure whether the exile caused him undue psychological damage but there is much to suggest that it did.

Ezekiel's call to prophecy which he readily accepts is unlike any other in biblical literature and has been the source of countless interpretations and analyses. It is not just the word of God that the prophet experiences but the hand of God resting upon him: a call of a uniquely physical nature.

Ezekiel's first, psychedelic vision, for it can hardly be thought of otherwise, has natural elements – ferociously strong winds, clouds and lightning – but it is what is supernatural that grabs our attention. He sees a huge cloud with a fiery aura and a fiery centre gleaming like amber in the middle of which he sees four figures that he labels as 'having the likeness of' human beings. This is important because what follows does not describe the sort of 'human figures' you would expect to see in other than your most terrible nightmares.

Each being has four faces, four wings with hands below the wings, and a single leg ending in a calf's hoof. One of the faces is a human, one a lion, one a bull and one an eagle. One pair of wings was for flying the other, it seems, for modestly covering their bodies. They can go in the direction that one face wants to go under their own propulsion, but they are also moved by the spirit (Hebrew: *ruach*) without any action on their own behalf. Within and around these extraordinary figures move lightning and fire, the biblical equivalent of strobe lighting.[cxvi]

In addition, each side of each being has a large wheel on it gleaming like beryl, a crystal that in its purest form is colourless; the wheel rims, described by Ezekiel as 'covered with eyes', are 'tall and awe-inspiring' and although the wheels appear to criss-cross each other, they move in the direction the creatures move whether on the earth or above it for the wheels are an organic part of the creatures.

Above them is a bright, gleaming ice-like substance from which emanates an extraordinary noise, like an army on the move or the crashing of seas. But above that what looks like a sapphire throne and on it a human being radiating an amber-like fire, calling to mind the wonder felt on seeing a rainbow. Ezekiel realises that he has seen the likeness of the glory of God, and immediately throws himself to the ground in a gesture of piety and awe.[cxvii]

[At this point a question comes to mind which needs to be answered – to which House of Israel is Ezekiel to address his message? It sounds as if it must be the Judahites in their own land, gradually sowing the seeds of their own collapse and destruction in 586, but how can it be Judah when Jeremiah is already there trying to save them? The answer is supplied by the text, clarifying that it is to the community in exile that Ezekiel is sent. Yet how can this be right – has the first deportation not been punished enough?

We cannot but infer from this that the first exiles, ripped from their land while its Temple still stood, considered themselves to be unfairly and poorly treated, a resentment that encourages them to act as they had 'back home'.

It is clear from Jeremiah's words of hope and reassurance about the aftermath of the exile that its purpose as punishment would only be achieved if the people returned to their covenant with God in a contrite spirit. If this had yet to be achieved no wonder Ezekiel was given a hard message to hammer home.]

Now the spirit that has moved the heavenly creatures and their wheels enters Ezekiel's body enabling him to hear the voice of God. The message, effectively Ezekiel's call to prophecy, is familiar; he is to prophesy to a rebellious people who have defied God's word, and not lose heart or be afraid when his words fall on deaf ears. But the task will be hard, likened to sitting on scorpions, the only time in the entire Hebrew Bible that such an image occurs.[cxviii]

To reinforce the message God gives him a scroll to eat which he does, describing it as tasting like honey, the best possible way apparently for Ezekiel to internalise God's message to the House of Israel. And finally God adds, as with Isaiah and Jeremiah, that however hard Ezekiel tries, however clear the message he gives to his people, they will not listen to him.[cxix]

In an instant Ezekiel feels himself lifted up and carried away, fired with zeal to deliver his message and surrounded by a colossal noise in which the words 'May God's glory be blessed from his place' echo, and then just as quickly finds himself set down in Tel Aviv by the Chebar tributary south of Babylon where the exiles are clustered. His response is to sit stunned on the ground for a whole week, not exactly what might have been expected.

Ezekiel is the only prophet who gets picked up and carried around and it is a moot point as to whether his sense that these things happened to him, never mind the nature of some of his visions most particularly the very first, are not the result of hallucinogenic drugs. There were several natural products that could result in spectacular trips: blue lotus, psylocibin mushrooms, qat, and opium for example, and it is not pushing the bounds of possibility too far to think that, for whatever reason, Ezekiel indulged and the visions duly followed.

In fact a great deal of Ezekiel's prophetic career seems centred on physical, symbolic gestures: being bound by cords, lying for very long periods on one side or another, eating food tainted with excrement, shaving his head and beard, clapping hands and stamping his feet.

He is transported by God to Jerusalem on more than one occasion, his wife dies but he is not allowed to mourn for her.[cxx]

Ezekiel's prophecies and oracles share much of the angry language of Jeremiah and he reinforces the sense of an utter degeneration of Judahite society and its betrayal of the covenant with God. There is the extra factor, however, of the weirdness Ezekiel brings to some of them, not least his apocalyptic visions introducing Gog and Magog, his grandiose delusions about a rebuilt Temple and a repetition of key commandments.[cxxi] It is not too fanciful to think that this implies that in some way Ezekiel saw himself as a reincarnation of Moses and Solomon!

But there is a darker aspect to Ezekiel that only becomes apparent as we read further into the book. He conceptualises the relationship between Jerusalem and God as being spousal with Jerusalem as the faithless wife; the prophet sexualises his imagery to a level unique in the Hebrew Bible (possibly excepting Song of Songs), not just apparently delighting in the images he draws but also in the behaviour he depicts, and going on and on in a similar vein until he details with an ill-concealed glee the violent punishment that she will suffer for her actions.[cxxii] And he repeats these images in a later oracle about two women named Oholah and Oholivah standing for the cities of Samaria and Jerusalem. There is an almost pornographic objectification of the women culminating in them being stoned to death and mutilated, their children destroyed with them. Later in the book Ezekiel is described as *shir (*emended to *shar) agavim*, a singer of bawdy songs, perhaps suggesting that his sexualised visions were listened to for reasons other than the ones he intended.[cxxiii]

We discern from the written text that this is all probably intended figuratively and Ezekiel sharing some of the cultural misogyny of other prophets should come as no surprise.

What is different about Ezekiel is that he seems to indulge more viscerally than other prophets, to delight not just in criticising his targets but in assaulting and humiliating them verbally. He sees no harm or reputational damage to God in ascribing this verbal violence to a divine source, and it is hard for us not to conclude that the God Ezekiel envisaged, and with whom he spoke, was an angry, vengeful and violent one with a particular hatred for women. And it is not too great a stretch to believe that this image of God does not actually represent the reality of the deity at all but rather Ezekiel's own, tortured thinking.

Many years ago I was taken to the art department of one of the UK's largest mental hospitals. I will never forget the images I saw that day, many of which showed distorted familiar images covered with eyes: I thought then of Ezekiel's opening vision and the chariot wheels covered with eyes; other pictures showed buildings drawn incredibly well and in minute detail, another connection with the prophet's plans for a rebuilt Temple in Jerusalem.

His oracles against the nations echo the venom of Jeremiah and Isaiah but go much further and in his vision of the slain in hell he lavishes the images with yet more horrific detail, apparently delighting in the death and destruction of those he calls *yordey vor*, 'those who have descended into the Pit'.[cxxiv]

Ezekiel's own apocalyptic visions are drenched in blood and death, an outpouring of horror that it is very hard to read with equanimity; so is there nothing in the book of Ezekiel that is not offensive, depressing or violent? The answer is yes, and although it does not mitigate the rest, it nevertheless gives us a glimpse of an Ezekiel of whom we otherwise see far too little.

The Vision of the Valley of the Dry Bones[cxxv] does, admittedly, start in an ancient battlefield covered in the skeletons of the dead. But when the dialogue between God and Ezekiel begins the situation improves dramatically.

'What do you see?' asks God. 'Very dry bones,' the prophet replies. 'Can these bones live again?' 'I haven't a clue,' Ezekiel responds. Then God tells him to prophesy over the bones and reassure them that God will bring them back to life, rebuilding their bodies and putting the breath of life into them that they may live and acknowledge God.

Ezekiel does as he is told and the great force of skeletons, rattling as they come together, are covered with sinews and flesh and skin, a vast inanimate host. Then God tells the prophet to call the four winds to breathe life into the bodies and it does so, and they rise up and stand.

What is the purpose of this miraculous act? The answer comes quickly. It is a *mashal*, a parable. The bones represent the forlorn hopes of the exiled House of Israel. They are depressed and desolate with no sense of relief in sight. But God has not abandoned them, God will revive them as if from the dead, God will restore them to their ancestral land and revive them as a people, and by this act all doubts about the existence and power of God will be laid to rest.

It is a stirring vision, for me the most powerful and meaningful of the entire book; if only it was the way the book ended! Unfortunately there are forty-eight chapters in Ezekiel so the feeling with which the reader is left is nowhere near as uplifting, or as benign towards the prophet as might otherwise be the case.

We are left with a deeply damaged man, some of the damage perhaps self-inflicted. A man whose displacement and exile in a foreign land have caused mental injury, but who is nevertheless chosen by God to be a prophet. His visions echo some of the shock and anger of exile, but they also indulge his baser feelings about his people, and about women, dressed up as divine communications.

For me, a significant clue is offered by Ezekiel's blueprint for a rebuilt Temple in Jerusalem and the puzzle as to why he creates this before the actual Temple has been destroyed? If we juxtapose him with his prophetic contemporary Jeremiah it is glaringly obvious that the latter does not indulge in such fantasies, even though he **has** seen the Temple destroyed. I can't help feeling that Jeremiah, who witnessed the destruction and was able to see it as an act of purification, raised his eyes to a grander vision of a future where the worship of God was no longer the preserve of the priestly classes. Ezekiel, an unwilling early deportee resentful of his exile, was able to blame the Temple and its abuse by the people, but could only envisage a future where another Temple, itself purified and led by a purified people, replaced the original.

There is much to dislike about Ezekiel, but seeing through him and his words to the horror of deracination and exile, the fair minded will find even more to pity.

MINOR PROPHETS

Chapter 9

The Twelve Minor Prophets

I: Hosea

Key text: The Book of Hosea
Date: 8th century BCE

Although it is a widely held view that the books of the twelve Minor Prophets were written after the fall of Jerusalem in 586 BCE, and most likely during the years of the Persian Empire (539–332 BCE), the book of Hosea is set firmly in the 8th century BCE, in the northern kingdom of Israel, against the backdrop of Assyria flexing its military muscles and threatening the entire region.

The book opens giving the period during which Hosea fulfilled his prophetic calling[cxxvi] echoing that of Isaiah and actually paralleling it making the two prophets, for a time, contemporaries. That apart, however, they do not have anything in common except their calling.

Much of the language of the book echoes canonically previous prophetic works and there are many similar images, but Hosea's prophetic career starts in an extraordinary way. Other prophets had to take drastic steps to bring their message home – let's not forget Isaiah spending three years naked – but Hosea's symbolic action is to marry a prostitute, Gomer, on God's instruction as a symbol of Israel's betrayal of its covenant with God and its whoring after others.[cxxvii]

Hosea is told to marry *eshet zenunim*, 'a wife of whoredom', and the word *zenunim* is in the plural suggesting that Gomer is not a part-time turner of

67

tricks but a full time professional. As a prostitute is by definition someone who sells her body for money to strangers, Hosea is being told to commit himself to someone whom, at the most intimate level, he will have to share. When he is told to have *yaldey zenunim* (children of prostitution) we must assume that the paternity of the son and daughter Gomer bears will at best be doubtful.[cxxviii]

This is an enormous commitment for Hosea to make, and one destined to give him a lot of grief, but he embraces it nevertheless.

The children are given symbolic names just like Isaiah's sons, the girl *Lo-ruhamah* (not pitied) and the boy *Lo-ammi* (not my people), further reinforcing the point that Hosea must make that just as the people of Israel and the kings that lead them have abandoned God, so will God mercilessly abandon them.

The instigation of Hosea's and Gomer's roles as representatives of the relationship between God and Israel, serves to cast Israel as a whore, using critical, misogynistic and violent language that is so distasteful in the book of Ezekiel. Some may see the reconciliation that is described here in a positive way, others may view it as the complete opposite – Hosea and his wife reconciling, and in so doing recalibrating their relationship in terms of the dominance of man over woman and the subjugation of a wife to her husband's will.

It appears from the text,[cxxix] in which many scholars identify an editor's heavy hand, that Hosea was told by God to have a relationship with another prostitute in addition to his wife, perhaps suggesting that Hosea, like some men in every stage of human history, was attracted to sex with women for whom it was a transaction rather than an integral part of a loving relationship between committed partners. Scholars do say, however, that this interpretation is stretching credulity a little too far, and that instead this is a re-writing of the original instruction to Hosea and refers to Gomer.

In addition to the repeated sex-related imagery, the verbal violence and loathing that typifies this short book, what is absent is a sense of the prophet. We may assume from the lack of any information about the impact on him of what he is told to do and say, that he had no moral or practical qualms whatsoever. Yet he must have done – with a wife on whom he could not rely and two children whose biological parent he might not have been – so perhaps he just never recorded them, applying to himself and his emotions the iron discipline and repression he seeks to impose on his wayward wife.

At the very end of the book (it is only fourteen chapters long) Hosea speaks words of tenderness, albeit not without some bite, foreseeing a time when Israel's sins will be forgiven because she will have accepted the wrong she did and the punishment she endured.[cxxx]

Perhaps this echoes a reconciliation of Hosea and Gomer, but we are not told; it is as if their lives were mere vehicles for a message, and once that has been communicated and understood they disappear, like vapour, into the mists of history.

II: Joel

Key text: The Book of Joel
Date: ca. 7th century BCE, possibly re-edited 5th–4th centuries BCE

It would be unlikely for a 21st century reader to give a work of only four chapters, and one of those very short, the title of 'book'; yet the books that are in the canon of the Hebrew Bible are there on merit and message rather than length.

The book of Joel, despite its diminutive size, is an important work for several reasons; it is not set in any particular historical period, although scholars take the reference to yevanim[cxxxi] (Greeks) as being indicative of a date sometime between 400 and 350 BCE, the period when Palestine was a province of the Persian Empire; others set it in its original form in the 7th century. Its author Joel ben Pethuel, though otherwise completely unknown, seems to be echoing other texts in his writing, indicative of a learned mind. It is the first book (chronologically at least) to focus on apocalyptic matters. And it contains more words for locusts than any other book in the Hebrew Bible!

Much of what Joel writes echoes the familiar themes of prophetic denunciation: the faithlessness of the people, the punishment that is coming, oracles against other nations, and a return to divine favour. But Joel does more than just eloquently echo the words of other prophets; he tackles a key theological misconception held by the people he addresses.

The 'Day of the Lord' is the moment when God intervenes again in human history, when the wicked will be judged and the righteous rewarded, and, depending which prophet is putting their own spin on the concept, is also a day of darkness and cosmic disturbance. The misconception is that the audience to whom Joel is addressing himself believe that they, as part of the House of Israel, will be part of 'the righteous' regardless of how they have behaved, and it is this delusion which the prophet is determined to correct.

Joel's Day of the Lord is one of havoc when a devastating famine will cover the land bringing disaster on man and beast alike, fires will consume the tinder dry ground, and darkness and gloom will descend upon the earth: but there is a way back.[cxxxii]

Joel tells the people that if they are whole-hearted not just in regret for past sins but actively repentant of them they will be forgiven.[cxxxiii] He mentions an edited version of the Thirteen Attributes of God spoken on Mt Sinai, identical to that found in the Book of Jonah, as a reminder of God's compassion and openness to a genuine change of heart.

Perhaps the most profound and lyrical part of the book of Joel comes at the start of chapter 3, when God promises to pour the Divine Spirit on all people, men and women, young and old, free and slaves. This will be a time when the dreams and visions that they enjoy will be on a level with those of the professionals (the prophets), when all will live a life of such virtue and moral worth as to be part of the remnant who will survive in Zion and Jerusalem when the great and terrible Day of the Lord comes that will shatter their enemies.[cxxxiv]

All stirring stuff, and for such a short book Joel receives the accolade of being read on the Sabbath before Yom Kippur, *Shabbat Shuvah*, the Sabbath of Repentance, because of its key themes of repentance and forgiveness.[cxxxv]

So what about the locusts? Why is Joel the biblical book with the largest amount of information about *Schistocerca gregaria*? Other prophets terrify with depictions of human armies and threats of what they will do when they attack, but for a largely agrarian population the army of locusts is even more frightening because it destroys their livelihoods, kills their animals through starvation and even puts at risk the people themselves. And Joel's locusts do not just appear as a fully formed swarm, there are grubs, hoppers, cutters and full-grown locusts, each stage needing to devour everything it can, the fourfold nature of the invasion meaning that absolutely nothing is left.[cxxxvi]

Why this image rather than a human army with swords and spears, chariots and bowmen? Because with a human army things can unexpectedly go wrong, your side may win through some strange quirk of fate; but there is no combatting a swarm that may have as many as forty to eighty billion insects in a square kilometre.

This makes Joel's imagery uniquely pitiless, and unforgettable.

III: Amos

Key text: The Book of Amos
Date: 8th century BCE

The Book of Amos is set squarely in the 8th century BCE during the long reigns of King Uzziah of Judah [783–735 BCE] and King Jeroboam II of Israel [786–746 BCE]. This was a time of stability, though Israel would fall to the Assyrians a mere twenty-four years after Jeroboam's death, and times of stability often lead to moral lassitude and societal corruption, prime territory for a prophet to step into.

The opening verse of the book gives us two intriguing details, one about timing, that he prophesied two years before "the earthquake" – an event we must assume of such magnitude that all who heard those words would know exactly the one referred to; and archaeological digs at the site of biblical Hazor have revealed evidence of a severe earthquake in 760 BCE. Apart from detailing the kings during whose reign Amos's prophetic stint took place, there is also mention of his profession - he is described as being *va-nokdim*, variously translated as 'among the herdmen'[KJV], 'one of the sheep-farmers' [NEB], 'among the shepherds' [NRSV], and 'a sheepbreeder' [NJV].[cxxxvii]

The issue thrown up by the differing translations seems to be what sort of a line of work was suitable for a prophet and would lend authority and gravitas to his role: the idea of Amos being a 'simple shepherd' was not good enough for some commentators and translators so the image of him actually following a flock of sheep had to be mitigated. Luckily, the word used in Amos is also used of the Moabite king Mesha, in that context meaning a breeder, or rancher of sheep, giving rise to Amos being similarly designated.[cxxxviii] This anti-shepherd snobbism seems strange when you bear in mind that having been a shepherd was one of the reasons why David was deemed suitable to be king.[cxxxix] If it was acceptable on the CV of the boy who became king why not for Amos?

Amos's principle preoccupation is the kingdom of Israel, an intriguing fact considering that his birthplace was in Judah in a village south of Bethlehem.

His oratorical style is considerable, his delivery seductive, and he draws his listeners closer and closer before hitting them with a harsh and unremitting message.

Amos's God is angry with everyone – Damascus, Gaza, Tyre, Edom, Ammon and Moab – their people all get it in the neck from Amos; one can imagine his listeners in Israel sitting or leaning back comfortably and enjoying the performance, and precisely at that point Amos says similarly damning things about Judah and finally Israel, and Israel's castigation is the longest of them all.[cxl]

Amos's ire is directed at moral iniquity, ritual transgression, material obsession and general depravity, familiar themes in prophetic literature;

what makes Amos's oracles so memorable is the language he uses, and some of his phrases are numbered among the most famous and familiar quotes from the Hebrew Bible. Amos reminds his listeners of what God has done for them, and the unique relationship they have with God, making their sins and failings all the more reprehensible, and he lays into the inhabitants of Samaria and depicts a terrible future for them.[cxli]

Like Jeremiah he is sarcastic when he needs to be, and he shares Isaiah's and Ezekiel's misogyny, though with an added edge of nastiness – he calls the women 'cows', blames them for the fact that their husbands are corrupt, and threatens them with a day when their corpses will be carried out of the city in baskets and thrown onto a rubbish heap[cxlii].

Amos does hold out a little hope for his people. In some of the grimmest denunciations he pauses, reminds the people that if they seek right and not wrong, practice justice and hate evil, God may well preserve a remnant of them, but such a passage is almost always an aside before he ploughs on with his message of doom and gloom.[cxliii]

His ire is at times expressed in familiar ways, but at others he rises to new heights, as when he ridicules those who hope that the Day of the Lord will be a day of salvation, describing it first as a day of darkness not light, but then toying with his listeners, telling them that the disappointment they will feel will be akin to a man who runs from a lion only to be attacked by a bear, and if he escapes and gets inside his own home rests his hand on the wall to catch his breath only to be bitten by a snake hidden in a crevice.[cxliv]

And if this isn't terrifying enough he adds that the Day of the Lord will not be one of mere darkness, but rather 'blackest night without a glimmer'.[cxlv]

Many years of studying the text of Amos leads me to feel that he is not just guilty of misogyny but also of misanthropy: his denunciations of the super-rich have an almost sensuous quality to them, as if he revels in the words he uses knowing that his targets have a terrible fate in store. It is as if on occasion he relishes the loathing he feels, a loathing which perhaps includes himself. Amos does have higher moments, when he seems to feel the pathos of what is coming for his people and asks God to refrain, using the memorable phrase, 'How will Jacob survive, he is so small?'[cxlvi] but they are the exception rather than the rule.

Another aspect of the Book of Amos that makes it very special is a short, biographical, tragi-comic encounter at the cult centre of Bethel, one of the two shrines in the northern kingdom of Israel set up by King Jeroboam I as competition to the Temple in Jerusalem. Unsurprisingly, Amos's loathing-filled diatribes aimed at the people of the kingdom and its king reach the ears of the authorities, in this specific instance Amaziah the priest of Bethel (probably the equivalent of Jerusalem's High Priest) and King Jeroboam himself, and they do not go down well.

In a confrontation which we should envisage in the sanctuary at Bethel Amaziah calls Amos a 'seer' rather than a prophet; the word for 'seer' in Hebrew, though sometimes appearing to be synonymous with the word for prophet, is a lesser term and here is meant to be derogatory and dismissive. 'Go back to Judah seer,' Amaziah says to Amos, 'and treat this place with respect, be a prophet elsewhere if you must!' Amos's response is intriguing. He says: 'I am not a professional prophet, nor a member of a prophetic guild, I am merely a herdsman and a horticulturalist (a dresser of sycamore figs). God told me to leave the flocks and prophesy, that is why I do this'.[cxlvii]

Amos as a breeder of cattle or sheep we have encountered before, but not the horticulturalist. What does a 'dresser of sycamore figs' do? It has been suggested that this refers to a manipulation of the process of pollination, making it certain rather than random, guaranteeing a greater yield of figs.

This suggests that Amos was very familiar with the countryside and all its growing cycles, knowledge that grounded him, connected him with the people who worked the land, and thus, perhaps, inspired him to be straightforward and open.

His answer to Amaziah has to say by implication, I am more engaged with what is really going on in this country than you are!

He follows up this response by damning the priest with a terrible prophecy, direct from God: 'You want me to stop? No! God's word to you is that your wife will become a whore, your children will be slaughtered, your land will be forfeit and you will die in exile'.[cxlviii]

The response of Amaziah is not recorded, and it is left to us to wonder whether he was enraged or terrified, but he is no longer relevant and so no more is heard of him.

The closing verses of the final chapter of Amos contain two important and unusually juxtaposed messages. The first is that of restoration, as with other prophets, and in spite of Amos's misanthropy there is some hope that the land and the people will be restored. He cannot, however, resist adding the sting that he is referring to the land of his birth, Judah, rather than Israel for whom there is no hope.

The second message is twofold and of enduring relevance: the fact that you have a covenant relationship with God doesn't make you any more special in God's eyes than the Ethiopians, the Philistines or the Arameans. God watches all peoples and lands and if they transgress they will be punished equally.[cxlix]

There is much in Amos which may be deemed not of lasting worth but this, for me at least, remains the overwhelming message. A relationship with God does not gift specialness, let alone superiority, to any individual or people; it has to be constantly worked for and earned. This is arguably a message of even greater importance today than at any time in Jewish history and one that we would be most unwise to ignore.

IV: Obadiah

Key text: The 'Book' of Obadiah
Date: 6th century BCE

I have put the word 'book' in inverted commas as it is hard to say whether one chapter of 21 verses, and no more than 291 Hebrew words, make a 'book' as we understand the word. Yet it was deemed worthy of inclusion in the biblical canon as a book and should therefore be taken seriously.

This does not require much effort for just beneath the literal meaning of the words is a greater and more lasting commentary.

Who was Obadiah? We haven't got a clue! There is an Obadiah mentioned in the first book of Kings[cl] but he is not in the right time period, being contemporary with King Ahab and his nemesis Elijah, nor is he described as a prophet. The rabbis mention this Obadiah several times but never to identify him with the biblical prophet, though there is an intriguing text in the Midrash[cli] which states that our Obadiah was an Edomite proselyte who prophesied against his own people; this is not a view substantiated by modern scholars.

So what did Obadiah prophesy against and when? The context for the book is post-586 BCE when the memories of the destruction of Jerusalem and its Temple by the Babylonians under Nebuchadnezzar, and the exile in Babylon that followed, were still very fresh in the minds of those who survived the cataclysm. The prophet cannot vent his grief, anger and bitterness against the Babylonians so he looks for a target closer to home, and he doesn't have to look too far.

Just over the other side of the Jordan was the kingdom of Edom, a people tracing their descent back to Esau the brother of Jacob who went to live in the region after he and Jacob had parted from each other.[clii] The Edomites were thus cousins to the Israelites and, however bad relationships may have been in the past or how much they ebbed and flowed, they were still family and as such should have stood by their family in times of crisis.

We know, however, that places where the greatest love resides can also be the source of the greatest hatreds. We know that estranged family members tend to have little to do with each other and even if one party is in crisis this often does not cancel estrangement or lead to reconciliation and support.

Obadiah's prophecy against Edom is not as vicious as it is because the Edomites failed to help the Judahites when the chips were down, but rather because they actually enjoyed the wrack of Jerusalem, the destruction of the Temple, and the killing of the city's defenders.[cliii] If that is not bad enough there is more: the Edomites not only celebrated the Babylonian action, they joined them in ransacking the city and set up road blocks on roads and paths so that Judean fugitives could be captured and handed over to the Babylonian army.[cliv]

These betrayals of the family bond motivate Obadiah to such an extreme of loathing that he prophesies the most horrible outcomes for Edom, returning the fate of the Judahites on their own heads but much worse. He is not alone; the author of Psalm 137 [By the rivers of Babylon...] describes the Edomites jeering from the side lines and urging the invaders to strip Jerusalem to its very foundations.[clv]

This background explains why the grudge evidenced in the book of Obadiah is as hard and cold and unremitting as it is, and it also explains something of much greater duration.

Due to its excoriation in Obadiah and elsewhere the kingdom of Edom became the archetypal Jewish enemy and Edom stood successively for those who oppressed the Jewish people, most notably the Roman Empire and Christianity. This happened long after Obadiah's time but it is hard to exaggerate the importance of his book in the process whereby Edom was transformed into a code word for something hateful in Jewish thought.

So why did the rabbis deem the one chapter book of Obadiah worthy of inclusion in the biblical canon? My answer is that its message about the depths to which familial relationships can plummet, and the hatreds that emerge from that awful abyss, is one to be taken very seriously and avoided at all costs: for that piece of timeless wisdom we have Obadiah to thank.

V: Jonah

Key text: The Book of Jonah
Date: ca. 4th century BCE

I will declare an interest at the start of this chapter because, although Jonah is not my favourite prophet, the Book of Jonah is my favourite prophetic book.

Some might be surprised to learn that there is any humour in the Hebrew Bible let alone comic incidents, but in the Book of Jonah there are several.

Jonah is Jonah ben Amittai, a prophet mentioned in the second book of Kings[clvi], who lived in the eighth century BCE during the long, stable and prosperous reign of King Jeroboam II of Israel. However convenient it would be to identify our Jonah with this namesake the chronology is against us. The Assyrian Empire under its king Tiglath-Pileser III only made serious inroads into the Middle East from about 745 BCE, a few years after the death of Jeroboam, and the city of Nineveh did not receive capital status until the reign of the Assyrian king Sennacherib (705–681BCE), let alone its reputation as the evil heart of an evil empire, which underlies the Book of Jonah, until a later date.

So it is probably wise to think of the Book of Jonah as a narrative, a piece of fiction which nevertheless is full of insights and feels very 'real'.

Jonah is spoken to by God without preamble or introduction and told to go to the capital of Assyria, Nineveh, and proclaim the city's destruction as punishment for their wicked ways. His response? To run in the opposite direction, get a berth on a ship crossing the Mediterranean, and avoid the mission completely. Unfortunately, you can neither run nor hide from God, and even though Jonah takes a bunk in steerage, right at the bottom of the boat, God knows precisely where he is and reacts accordingly.[clvii]

A fearful storm erupts, so ferocious that the crew think the ship will capsize. The crew go down to the depths of the boat where he has been deeply asleep, and the captain roughly rouses him and tells him to pray to his god to bring an end to the storm. In their fear and confusion about what is happening the sailors cast lots to see who might, in whatever way, be responsible. The lot as we might expect falls on Jonah.

'Who on earth are you?' they enquire, 'why are you here and what have you done?'[clviii]

The answer Jonah gives is not exactly designed to pacify them: 'I am a Hebrew,' he says, 'and the God I worship is the God of heaven and earth.'

78

The terror that engulfs the sailors is no surprise, but they are decent people and ask him what he has done to earn God's displeasure; so he tells them about his divine commission and they ask what needs to be done to still the storm.

When he tells them that throwing him in the sea should have the desired effect, rather than following his suggestion they redouble their efforts to bring the ship to safety but to no avail. Then they pray to Jonah's God for absolution and throw Jonah overboard. Instantly the storm ends and with it the swell. And what is the sailors' first response? To pledge allegiance to God and offer him a sacrifice. If Jonah hadn't been in the sea he would have known that this was his first success, and it might have done more than hint to him that try as he might he was not going to evade God's charge.[clix]

Unfortunately for Jonah, he couldn't know what had happened on board because he was in the stomach of a large fish that had swallowed him on God's instruction. Although most people describe the large 'fish' as a 'whale', probably thanks to the original Jewish translation of the Hebrew Bible into Greek (Septuagint) which used 'great sea monster', it is definitely a fish.

No need to waste time protesting that no fish could swallow a man whole, or that whales are not to be found in the Mediterranean (they are), or that if swallowed no human being could survive, because we are dealing with a story albeit one with a profound practical and spiritual purpose.

Jonah prays fervently to God from the fish's belly and, again commanded by God, the fish chokes up Jonah on the shore where he barely has time to dry off before God repeats the original command to go to Nineveh and proclaim its coming destruction. This time Jonah obeys without question having clearly accepted that further resistance is futile.

At this stage we know nothing of Jonah's inner thoughts, but almost immediately something extraordinary happens; the citizens of the city, the king, even livestock, put on sackcloth, fast, and repent sincerely for all their wrongs. In response God forgives them and stays the punishment. Job done.

You might expect Jonah to be pleased, but you would be wrong. He is angry and resentful, and then he gives God a tongue lashing: 'I knew this is what you'd do. You have form as a God of mercy and compassion, renouncing punishment where there is sincere repentance.'[clx] 'That's why I ran away, you didn't need me at all, you could have accomplished it all alone.' Then he adds for good measure, 'I've had it, kill me now.'[clxi]

God's response is quiet, and when I read it, I hear an audible smile, 'Are you sure you're right to be angry?'

Jonah is in such a sulk that he doesn't even answer, leaves the city, puts up a temporary shack and sits in it waiting to see what transpires. God then teases him by making a shade-giving plant grow over the hut in the night so that the following day Jonah has shade and it lifts his spirits. But that evening God commissions a worm to chew through the roots so that the plant withers and dies, exposing Jonah to full sun, and adding a sultry east wind to make his situation even harder[clxii].

Jonah suffers now in a way he has not before and he says to God again, 'I am fed up with life, let me die.' And God repeats quietly, 'Are you sure you're right to be angry about the plant?' To which Jonah replies with some vehemence, 'Yes, I'm so upset I've had enough.'[clxiii]

And with these words we hear no more from Jonah, but we do hear from God: 'You didn't nurture or grow the plant you cared for and it only lasted twenty-four hours, so should I not care about Nineveh, a city of one-hundred and twenty thousand clueless people, not to mention many animals?'[clxiv]

It is a magical rhetorical question on which to end this prophetic book, the only book in the entire Hebrew Bible to end with a question.

What then are the principal themes of Jonah? Where God is concerned you can neither run nor hide, for sure. That God accepts those who sincerely repent their sins, the same.

But what the Book of Jonah also tells us is that divine concern is not restricted to believers, in the context of his audience Israelites, in ours Jews, but extends to all peoples. This is a positive message but also a challenging one, because it implies that God watches over everything and everyone, which has profound implications for personal behaviour.

And what follows from this is the inherent truth that God is not restricted to one group of people or one particular country or area, but is universal, a huge theological step forward from the idea of national deities.

There is something else, however, which makes the Book of Jonah uniquely special. We are used to God talking to prophets, and we are quite used to prophets talking to God, but none of them appears to have the relationship with God that Jonah enjoys.

God is like a father to Jonah who neither terrifies nor over-awes him. He talks to God just like he would talk to anyone else, not because he is contemptuous, rude, or arrogant, but because he knows God, understands how God works in the world, and from a position of respect loves God too. God is clearly fond of Jonah; there is no need for the pyrotechnics laid on for Moses at Mt Sinai, the flashy visions of Ezekiel, or the dynamic miracles of Elijah, the relationship is quiet and almost laid back.

Jonah has no fear of showing his feelings, he wears them on his sleeve for God to see, and when he feels petulant or sulky or angry he admits it, seeing no sense in pretending to a God who knows his innermost thoughts. And when God toys with Jonah it is done to explain not to harm or punish.

We are left with a question at the end of the Book of Jonah, but its key themes, not to mention its pivotal relationship, are what linger with us long after the final page has been turned.

VI: Micah

Key text: The Book of Micah; Jeremiah 26.18
Date: 8th century BCE

The prophet Micah is an eighth century BCE prophet, contemporary with Isaiah, and his short book is particularly known for two extracts, the first states:[clxv]

In the days to come,
The Mount of the Lord's House shall stand
Firm above the mountains:
And it shall tower above the hills.
The peoples shall gaze on it with joy,
And the many nations shall go and shall say:

"Come,
Let us go up to the Mount of the Lord,
To the House of the God of Jacob;
That He may instruct us in His ways,
And that we may walk in His paths."
For instruction shall come forth from Zion,
The word of the Lord from Jerusalem.

The former parallels but does not exactly replicate Isaiah 2.2–4[clxvi], and it is much debated as to which preceded which. Comparing the two, their differences remind me of a piece of work plagiarised by a pupil who has changed one or two words and altered the order of others, in an attempt to make 'theirs' different from the original.

Is one better than the other? This is a very subjective matter, but I think that of Isaiah resonates better, although what follows the Micah version presents one of those haunting images of a future that might be but which we will probably never achieve: when 'everyone shall sit under their vine and under their fig tree and none shall make them afraid.'[clxvii]

Almost anyone familiar with the Hebrew Bible, or the Old Testament, knows the second extract:

He has told you, O man, what is good,
And what the Lord requires of you:
Only to do justice
And to love goodness
And to walk modestly with your God.

So who was Micah, who from the two quotes above we might think of as a slightly gentler prophet than his peers? All we know about him from the Bible is the place of his birth, Moreshet-Gat, an ancient village mentioned in Egyptian documents dating from the fifteenth and fourteenth centuries BCE and close to Lachish, a fortified town that fell to the Assyrians in 701 BCE during Micah's lifetime.

The seven chapters that comprise Micah's book contain several prophecies elements of which chime with those of other prophets, and it is hardly surprising that such individuals would have similar responses to events on a national and supra-national scale which they believed would have profound implications for their own people. It must surely be the case that just as the prophets knew what could go right in a proper covenant relationship between Israel and God, so they had a common view of what was going wrong; and perhaps they also read the signs well enough to be confident that calamity was coming, and with it potential theological fallout for that covenant relationship? Micah castigates both Israel and Judah for their faithlessness and idolatry – the immoral and amoral, the leaders of the people, the false prophets – and prophesises doom and destruction for them all, though without quite the relish of other prophets.[clxviii]

But the last two chapters add fresh elements. Micah writes as if we are in a court of law: God is the prosecuting barrister and Micah speaks for the defence; Israel is in the dock. This is a dynamic and powerful scenario: God summons the ancient parts of the earth as a jury, and sets out the case for the prosecution, outlining the great acts God has performed for the people, making their abandonment of the covenant even more reprehensible and unforgivable.

Micah, speaking for the defence, asks a series of rhetorical questions about what it is that God requires, answering them with that splendid statement about justice, mercy and walking modestly with God. If it was a final argument it would be a clincher, but God is not finished; another charge follows, more bitter than the first.

In the face of this onslaught the defence collapses and Micah throws himself on the mercy of the jury (especially as the judge looks suspiciously like the prosecutor), presenting an image of moral and societal destitution, adding, perhaps on behalf of the righteous remnant who are always around somewhere, that they will wait patiently for God to save them; getting no interruption he continues laying it on with a trowel. 'My enemy taunts me, claiming that my God has abandoned me,' he says; 'but God will vindicate me and punish those who hate me, becoming once again my light and my champion.'[clxix]

And finally, in the closing verses the mood changes completely, looking to the future with confidence and hope, and a certainty that God will gather Israel in and forgive their sins.

Micah thus presents us with a series of messages, some predictable, parallels of others in prophetic literature, yet others very different, and concludes with an upbeat message that only a cynic would deem not an integral part of the book.

And there is one more thing to note about Micah – that he is the *Tashlikh* prophet. *Tashlikh* is a symbolic ceremony that takes place after the morning service on the first day of Rosh Hashanah. Jews gather at a body of water, emptying their pockets into the water as a sign of ridding themselves of sin at the start of a new year. And the words recited at this moment are those of Micah:[clxx]

> *He will take us back in love;*
> *He will cover up our iniquities,*
> *You will hurl all our sins*
> *Into the depths of the sea.*

Although a minor prophet, Micah's connections with the holiest time of the Jewish year, as well as his most important message about right human conduct, served to keep him close to the forefront of Jewish minds and hearts and will long continue so to do.

VII: Nachum

Key text: The Book of Nachum
Date: ca. 7th century BCE

The opening words of the book of Nachum warn the reader that this is a strange prophetic book, one that is different from others: *An oracle concerning Nineveh. The book of the vision of Nachum of Elkosh.* How? Because it begins, not with the prophet's name, but rather with the subject of the prophecy. The prophet's name takes second place enforcing the point that this prophecy has a singular focus and the prophet himself is purely a vehicle for the message. The prophet's name is Nachum, and he is called the Elkoshite indicating the place of his birth as Elkosh the precise location of which remains a mystery.

How are we to date Nachum? The words around the sack of Nineveh are so graphic that some assume they must have been written shortly after the city's destruction in 612 BCE; others think that the reference to the Egyptian city of Thebes/No-Amon which was captured by the Assyrians in 663 provide a time bracket for the writing of the book. It is further thought that the text was edited in post-exilic times. Whether it is a brilliant piece of prophecy or a brilliant piece of literature or just a hopeful piece of vitriol doesn't matter that much for the content, aspects of which are timeless, counts much more than the date of its writing.

The target is the city of Nineveh, previously encountered in the Book of Jonah, but there is no benignity here, no universal God with compassion for all peoples and open to their repentance. In Nachum, God is a force of terrible destruction, a vengeful God coming to punish Nineveh for its arrogance and its imperial and hubristic actions throughout the ancient Middle East.

The tone is set with the first words of the prophecy: God is angry, and God is vengeful, and the word vengeful (*nokem* in Hebrew) is repeated three times in one verse, an almost unparalleled repetitiousness in the Hebrew Bible.

Then there is a twist, Nachum echoes but distorts a text from Exodus that would have been known to an Israelite audience, where the Thirteen Attributes of God are listed.[clxxi]

Nachum mentions God's patience and forbearance but ignores other attributes such as graciousness and mercy because this is not the God of whom he speaks; God's mighty lovingkindness is replaced by mighty power and then comes the killer punch, that God does not remit all punishment, echoing the Exodus text.

The juxtaposition of these things and their alteration makes it very clear that Nachum's message to Nineveh is one completely lacking in hope. There is no chance whatsoever that anything they can do will alter God's course and the coming destruction, payback for all Assyria's deeds.[clxxii]

Nachum then lists the global power of God, his ability to make 'the mountains quake and the hills to melt' before gradually tightening the focus to the city, its siege and then destruction together with the people within it. Juxtaposed with this gloom, mayhem, ruin and human suffering set out in almost loving detail, there is a little about Israel, acknowledging how it will rejoice at Nineveh's suffering and feel its lost pride restored by God.[clxxiii]

The central narrative is written in extraordinary staccato Hebrew and works on the reader rather like a piece of music whose beat builds to a great crescendo taking the heartbeat of the listener to a similar high. This text heightens vindictive anticipation and *schadenfreude* in equal measure as one vicious and terrible image is piled onto another, just as the anticipated corpses in Nineveh will be stacked up.[clxxiv]

No other book in the entire Hebrew Bible possesses imagery as stark, unremitting and terrible as that in Nachum, nor any in literary terms as effective: the book ends not on a high note, for there is no hope for Nineveh, it ends on the lowest note possible.[clxxv] The Hebrew text reads: *Al mi lo avrah ra-atcha tamid;* translated in the NJV as, 'For who has not suffered from your constant malice?' The NRSV says, 'For who has ever escaped your endless cruelty?'and the NEB has, 'Are there any whom your ceaseless cruelty has not borne down?'

It seems appropriate that a book delighting in its unashamed malice towards a bitter enemy should end with the word malice, as the NJV translates, but there is a grammatical twist which makes the last two Hebrew words capable of two translations. In Hebrew, possessive suffixes have a dual meaning in some cases; they can indicate possession by, or that which is attributable to, the possessor. This gives us the possibility of another translation which may be closer to the meaning intended by this angriest of prophets – 'the malice which is owed to you shall never pass away!'

VIII: Habakkuk

Key text: The Book of Habakkuk
Date: ca.7th–6th centuries

This is another of the shorter prophetic books that gives us no clues about the identity of the prophet – we only have his name – or the date that the book was written. It is believed by scholars, however, to have been written after the Assyrian Empire fell to the Babylonians in 612 BCE and before Jerusalem fell in 586. The Babylonians, who are called Chaldeans by Habakkuk, are clearly a growing threat, for an answer to which Habakkuk entreats God, without success.

Divided into three chapters, the first two take the form of a dialogue between God and the prophet, the last is a *tefillah*, a prayer, though stylistically it is a psalm.

The book opens with the word *ha-masa*, which literally means 'the burden', and is yet another word used in connection with prophecy. Though it is translated as 'the pronouncement' by the NJV, retaining the word 'burden' (linked to their prophecies by others such as Isaiah and Jeremiah) gives it an undertone of dread.

This is enhanced by the opening of chapter one: Habakkuk is fearful of what is clearly to come and asks God how long he will be impervious to cries for help, suggesting that uncertainty and the fear it creates are causing normal society to break down.[clxxvi]

God's response to this plea is not comforting. The approaching danger is not a random thing; it is an instrument of divine anger. God describes the Babylonian hordes in chilling terms likening their horses to leopards and wolves and their search for plunder of all kinds as akin to vultures.[clxxvii]

Habakkuk's response is rather combative: he tells God that he is a God of righteousness, that having existed for eternity he has by implication overseen all sorts of human frailty, but has never been unjust. The implication is that the current situation is unjust and God must come to Israel's aid. The image that he uses is that of a trawler man taking great trouble to pull in a good catch but then emptying his net and letting all the fish go. You need to hang on to us, Habakkuk seems to say, you've put enough effort into hauling us in! And he asserts that he won't move from the spot until he gets an answer.[clxxviii]

God's reply is a surprise: 'Write this down on tablets so that it can be read easily by others.'[clxxix] The only other prophet who writes down prophecies, albeit in a scroll rather than inscribed on tablets, is Jeremiah,[clxxx] making this instruction unusual and significant. In an age when almost everything other than legal transactions was oral, the writing down of a prophecy implies that it should have a real permanence and can be disseminated much more widely than might otherwise be possible.

The major part of God's response is directed externally at the enemy rather than at Israel, explaining why it needed to be written down as it would need to be carried some distance to reach them in their own land.

The third and final chapter is Habakkuk's prayer, and it is given an apparently musical accompaniment on *Shigyonot*, though we cannot be sure what the word means or whether it refers to a musical instrument or a style of music. It is a psalm in the petitionary style, asking God to do something specific, to be precise, to manifest his power as in former times. The prophet details the steady progress of the Divine Presence preceded and followed in awful power by plague and pestilence. The tone is not only cosmic it is earthly, spelling out not just what will happen in the heavens but also the military havoc to be wreaked on earth.[clxxxi]

It concludes on a note of steadfast faith regardless of the fact that the land is ruined; Habakkuk rejoices in his God who is his strength and deliverer.

The little book of Habakkuk, however, bound by its content to a specific time or so we might have thought, has two more little surprises.

The first is the fact that chapter 2.3b, 'if he delays, wait for him; for he will surely come, he will not delay' has become a fundamental text linked to the doctrine of the coming of the Messiah, a mantra no less a person than Moses Maimonides made one of his thirteen principles of faith.[clxxxii] Whether this is the intention of the verse ultimately matters little for, deracinated from its source, it has taken on a life of its own.

The second takes us to the Dead Sea Scrolls. Among the scrolls of the Qumran community that have been identified and analysed, and which may be seen online, are several fragments of commentary by the sect on certain biblical books, among them Habakkuk. The purpose of the sect in writing commentary on these texts was to extract meaning and relevance to their own time, and the Pesher Habakkuk, which was among the first such commentaries to be found, was clearly a rich source for them.

The unknown author interprets the Chaldeans as representing the Romans who had imposed rule on Judea in 63 BCE, and other references are interpreted as referring to two key figures in Qumranite theology, the Teacher of Righteousness and the Wicked Priest. The Habakkuk commentary refers to the Romans being invited into the land by 'the advice of a family of criminals', usually taken to refer to the Hasmonean ruling family, descendants of Judah the Maccabee and his brothers. [140–63 BCE]

This footnote to the book of Habakkuk is a reminder that such biblical texts, which have always been a rich source of rabbinic interpretation and commentary, were a vehicle for much earlier interpretation by small sects not within the Jewish mainstream, giving them a relevance and contemporaneity their original authors can never have envisaged.

IX: Zephaniah

Key text: the Book of Zephaniah
Date: 7th century BCE

If you are hoping for some light relief after the assault on the senses that Nachum and Habakkuk represent, Zephaniah will prove a disappointment, at least until close to the end of the final chapter.

Many of the common themes in other prophetic texts are to be found in Zephaniah: the Day of the Lord is coming but it will be a day of punishment rather than reward, a day of anger, calamity, and desolation. Judah is in trouble but so are nations round about and Zephaniah homes in on specific cities that will also feel the measure of divine wrath. They are to be punished not for their idolatrous worship or internal immorality but for the way they have treated Judah, the possession of God's people Israel.[clxxxiii]

Four of the five Philistine cities, regular prophetic targets like the kingdoms of Moab and Ammon on the east bank of the Jordan rising to a crescendo of doom for Assyria and the desolation of Nineveh, all feel the lash of Zephaniah's tongue.[clxxxiv] The last may cause no surprise when taken in the context of the previous books, but it is noteworthy in view of the way this book commences.

Unlike Nachum and Habakkuk, about whom their books tell us nothing, the lineage of Zephaniah is given back to his great-great grandfather and we are told that his period of prophecy was during the reign of King Josiah.[clxxxv] Josiah ruled from 640 to 609 BCE, ascending the throne as a child of eight when his father Amon was assassinated. His death at the age of 39, after a reign which saw major religious reforms and promised much more, was a tragedy which profoundly affected Josiah's contemporaries Jeremiah and Zephaniah. He died, quite unnecessarily, by engaging in battle with Pharaoh Necho II at Megiddo as the latter was passing through Judah to fight with the Assyrians against the Babylonians. Necho had no fight with Josiah and yet, when challenged at Megiddo, had superior forces which won the day.

It was a waste of a life, a waste of an opportunity that might significantly have brought stability and common sense to the whole history of Judah, and potentially to Jewish history thereafter.

The impact of Josiah's death on Zephaniah inspired the vitriol he heaps on Nineveh, as a cipher for Assyria as a whole, clearly blaming the Assyrians for indirectly causing Josiah's demise and revelling in Nineveh's destruction and the death and deportation of its people.[clxxxvi]

Zephaniah's description of a great city laid waste and steadily being claimed by the desert, its ruins the home of wild animals and birds, suggests to me that he had seen such a place and used the memory to enrich his own imagery;[clxxxvii] perhaps the city of Samaria itself, sacked by the Assyrians in 722, its inhabitants exiled to oblivion, members of the ten tribes of Israel lost for all time?

Zephaniah mentions more birds and animals in his book than any other prophet – jackdaws, owls, ravens, lions and wolves – and we may wonder whether he had an acute eye for nature or wandered widely and had seen the creatures he names or both. Whatever the truth he uses them to good effect.[clxxxviii]

Another intriguing aspect of Zephaniah is the ambiguity that underpins some of his pronouncements: the reader thinks he is speaking about Nineveh, yet there is a possibility that he is really referring to Jerusalem. Perhaps in the aftermath of Josiah's death Zephaniah felt that the likelihood of his reformation taking a deep hold on the kingdom and its people was diminished if not fatally damaged and he foresees what will happen as an inevitable outcome of a slide back into idolatry and the abuse of Temple ritual.

This ambiguity is an unusual aspect of the book, being a strong rhetorical device not widely found in the Hebrew Bible, the prophets usually being unequivocal about what they meant. As such it works very well here and would certainly have kept his audience's attention.

The last nine verses of the book are a wonderful evocation of a restored Jerusalem, its time of punishment over, its future bright, God intimately woven into the fabric of the city and its people, the promises made to Abraham [Gen.22.17-18] finally fulfilled.[clxxxix]

Upbeat conclusions to biblical books whose tenor is altogether darker are not uncommon. Some look clumsy, as if added by an editor who felt that the original ending was too stark or grim, but there is something transformative about the conclusion of the book of Zephaniah as if the prophet has looked into the future and seen something good and positive. It is an ending which endears this little known prophet to me and makes me wish more were familiar with his work and his words.

X: Haggai

Key text: The Book of Haggai
Date: 6th century BCE

The book of Haggai is so short – only two verses longer than Obadiah – that it is often paired with that of Zechariah which follows it; these two together with the book of Malachi are the last of the twelve Minor Prophets.

Several factors, however, mark Haggai out as being special. First, in a slew of prophetic books largely written in biblical Hebrew poetry Haggai is written entirely in prose. Second, because the prophecies it contains are post-exilic and post-destruction; God has punished Israel and decreed the Temple's demolition, now the prophet foreshadows its rebuilding.[cxc] Third, unlike his prophetic predecessors Haggai is partnered by the Jewish civil and religious authorities and the people listen to him! Fourth, we can date precisely Haggai's prophecies. Fifth, it ends on a note which seems to suggest the restoration of the Davidic monarchy.[cxci]

There are four narrative pronouncements in Haggai dated as follows: first, the 1st of Elul in the second year of King Darius I (520 BCE); the second on the 21st of Tishri, the third on the 24th of Kislev, and the fourth on the same day, all in the same year. This dating has all the hallmarks of the precise Persian bureaucracy and can be seen to be squeezed into a four-month period.[cxcii]

Haggai is in the thick of plans for rebuilding the Temple, and plays a significant part in strengthening the will of Zerubbabel the governor and

Joshua the High Priest as they seek to re-erect God's house on its original site. We know that those returnees from exile who remembered the original pre-586 BCE structure, considered its post-exilic successor to be a pale imitation. Haggai encourages them to tackle the matter head on and have faith, because above all else is the not inconsiderable fact that God is with them. Just like the Exodus from Egypt God is happy with the efforts they are making, and he promises a bumper crop and harvest as a further sign of divine pleasure.

These are different images from the prophetic norm and hugely refreshing as a result.

Haggai's final prophecy is the shortest, a mere four verses speaking of military force being rendered completely redundant for Zerubbabel has been designated as God's signet ring and chosen by God. It is a glorious conclusion, a statement of royal restoration that is not part of a messianic future but of the here and now.[cxciii] It is the most upbeat possible note on which to end.

XI: Zechariah

Key text: the Book of Zechariah
Date: 6th century BCE

Zechariah lived at the same time as Haggai during the first few years of the reign of the Persian king Darius I. Zechariah's prophetic career begins in the autumn of 520 BCE and his father Berechiah and grandfather Iddo are named when he is introduced in the opening verse of the book; this is more biographical information than we have about all the other Minor Prophets with the exception of Zephaniah.

His visions and prophecies focus like the more prosaic Haggai on the rebuilding of the Temple after the Persian-permitted return from Babylonian exile. Yet the content of his book which runs to fourteen chapters could hardly be more different. Indeed Zechariah while sharing characteristics with all the other prophetic books differs from them in one significant way, the first six chapters being comprised largely of visions which are explained not by God but by an angel who mediates God's word to the prophet.[cxciv]

The mood of these chapters is perhaps predictably somewhat ethereal; Zechariah sees a man mounted on a bay horse with three other horses behind him in a grove of myrtle. He sees four horns, four blacksmiths, a man holding a measuring line, and the High Priest Joshua (named in the book of Haggai) standing before the angel of the Lord together with the accusing angel called *ha-Satan* in Hebrew, but definitely not meaning the Satan of Christianity. Joshua is dressed in filthy clothes which are removed once the accusing angel has been rebuked and he is dressed again in beautiful priestly garments. He sees a golden menorah set between two olive trees, a flying scroll, a measuring vessel with a lead stopper in which a woman sits, two women with stork wings who carry off the vessel, four chariots drawn by horses of different colours, and none of them does he understand.[cxcv]

So he asks the angel and the angel explains what each of the visions symbolises, most of them being taken to indicate events of restoration – religious and national and the revivification of dignity – culminating in chapter six with the re-consecration of Joshua as the High Priest indicating the Temple's restoration and accompanying religious self-determination.

These themes are understandable in the context of the restoration of the Babylonian exiles to Judah, now the Persian province of Yehud, and the plans to rebuild the Temple and with it the city of Jerusalem. The events of the early decades of the sixth century BCE had a profound existential and spiritual impact on the returnees, and the trauma of homecoming could easily have been as traumatic as that of exile. Being forcibly removed from your home is terrible, but so is returning to it years later and seeing the changes that have occurred without you witnessing or being in any way involved with them.

This psychic disturbance may go some way to explaining the strange almost obtuse nature of Zechariah's visions; perhaps he is unable to see the meaning because he is prevented from thinking clearly by the calamities he and his people have experienced, or having the confidence of pre-exilic prophets to interpret correctly. Although God is showing him the visions there is no direct divine conversation, rather God talks to the angel who then communicates with the prophet.

The Angel of the Lord, *Mal-ach Adonai* in Hebrew, is unnamed in the book of Zechariah, setting up an intriguing mystery as to its identity. Searches through rabbinic literature do not provide the conclusive answer that we might wish, but perhaps through analogy with the prophet Daniel who has a similarly complex and otherwise inexplicable vision clarified for him by an angel, named as the archangel Gabriel,[cxcvi] it is Gabriel who plays an identical role for Zechariah. (This also sets off intriguing thoughts about whether the story of Gabriel revealing Allah's will to Mohammed in the Qur'an is yet another example of Jewish influences on the early traditions of Islam, known as *israilyat* in Arabic.)

Chapters 7 and 8 are like 1 to 6 written in prose, but with chapter 9 a mixture of poetry and prose typifies the content of the remaining chapters.

The final chapter brings us back to familiar territory, the Day of the Lord, except that it has elements that are not found in other prophetical writing on the same subject.

To start with, all the nations will come to attack Jerusalem, will capture the city plunder its contents and rape its women, and some of its citizens will be taken into exile, but only some for the rest will be allowed to remain. God will then attack the attackers smiting them with a horrible plague and vanquishing them. The honour of Jerusalem and its citizens will be restored and all the nations shall come to Jerusalem on a pilgrimage once a year for the festival of Sukkot, and if they do not come it is they who will be punished for their ritual dilatoriness.[cxcvii]

The chapter, and with it the book, ends in an extremely mundane way talking about the ritual purity of cooking pots beyond the Temple precincts and the absence of *che-na-ani*, a Hebrew word variously translated as 'traders'[NJV/NRSV/NEB] or 'Canaanite' [KJV].[cxcviii] [In spite of the fact that the NJV says of the word 'meaning of Hebrew uncertain' there are sufficient occurrences elsewhere of the Hebrew *ke-na-ani* clearly meaning 'merchant' or 'trader' as to minimise the uncertainty.]

There is more, however, to the book of Zechariah than his strange visions. The text contains some phrases which have become part and parcel of Jewish literature in their own right.

The opening verses of chapter 4 mention a seven-branched candlestick and are selected as the Haftarah reading for the Sabbath that occurs during the festival of Chanukkah; it contains the phrase, 'Not by might nor by power but by My spirit says the Lord of Hosts'.[cxcix] The festival celebrates the Maccabean uprising in the middle of the second century BCE when the Jews fought and conquered an overwhelming force and regained their religious and practical independence.

The quote harmonises well with the story found in the first and second books of Maccabees in the Apocrypha, which gives as much credit to God for the Maccabean victories if not more than the human armies. It has also been a mantra over the centuries for Jews desperate for relief from oppression, helping to keep alive the hope that God's power is greater than any human being's and could yet achieve miracles.

Another aspect that sets Zechariah apart from the major prophets is the mixture of apocalyptic/messianic material.

Several prophets talk about the Day of the Lord and the sections of Isaiah that have a messianic ring to them are unforgettable, but Zechariah manages to paint a picture in wonderful rich colours of a Zion and Jerusalem not just at peace with themselves but with all the world, and containing a verse whose Christological interpretation has played a significant role in Christian thought and iconography:

> *Rejoice greatly, Fair Zion; raise a shout Fair Jerusalem!*
> *Lo, your king is coming to you. He is victorious, triumphant,*
> *yet humble, riding on an ass, on a donkey foaled by a she-ass.*[cc]

though it is doubtful that Zechariah had the image of Jesus in mind when these words were spoken.

The final major aspect of Zechariah is that in the book's penultimate chapter he specifies the end of the prophets,[cci] saying that God will cause prophets to disappear from the land, that being a prophet will be taboo, and taking a sideswipe at Elijah and Amos as he does so ('he will not wear a hairy mantle', 'I am a tiller of the soil'). This piece of text at least to start with could refer to false prophets as fulminated against by Amos and Jeremiah among others; but the mention of the item of clothing synonymous with Elijah and the apparent allusion to Amos suggests that all prophets are included,[ccii] and the rabbis seem to have understood it this way, being of the view that the Divine Spirit left the Jewish people after the death of Malachi.[cciii][BT Yoma 9b]

This may be interpreted in another way, however, for prophecy has existed in every human generation. To my pragmatic view the rabbis saw the prophets as exceptional men of the past to whom God spoke directly, but in their own time God did not appear to speak to anyone other perhaps than echoes heard by the rabbis, and the rabbis' role was to interpret Jewish law which was what bound people to a common cause and a common faith. The last thing they needed was individuals standing up and proclaiming that they had received word direct from God which contradicted what the rabbis were doing or saying. So they fastened with gratitude on the relevant verses in Zechariah chapter 13 and said that prophecy ended with him, Haggai and Malachi.

XII: Malachi

Key text: The Book of Malachi
Date: late 5th century BCE

The rabbis dealt with the fact that Malachi is mentioned at the start of the book bearing his name without any patronymic or indication of his family by suggesting that it was a nom-de-plume for Ezra, but that smacks to me of desperation and I would prefer to take the text at face value and imagine a prophet otherwise unnamed and dubbed Malachi, meaning 'My messenger'. He would appear to date to a time after the return from exile and the rebuilding of the Temple so that his words were addressed to Jewish subjects of the Persian Empire living in the Persian province of Yehud.

The single pronouncement of Malachi is spread over three chapters, and in 2.11 there is a clue to it being post-exilic when it refers to Judah having 'espoused daughters of alien gods',[cciv] and we know from the books of Ezra[ccv] and Nehemiah[ccvi] that intermarriage with pagan locals by those who had remained in Judah greatly exercised the leadership of the returnees.

Many of the themes in Malachi are familiar: a stern patriarchal God looks at his people disappointed by their failure to do as they have been instructed, hurt by their disloyalty yet promising to stick by them all the way to a final liberation.[ccvii] Malachi is concerned with those who flout Temple rituals, with those who break marriage vows and those who twist teachings of truth into falsehood.

Then in the final chapter the text takes a dramatic and unexpected turn. God will send 'My messenger' who shall herald some unprecedented events: the angel of the covenant is coming but is coming to purify like a smelter's fire and all those who have betrayed God will be punished. God's own words echo out to the people demanding a wholesale reformation in behaviour before there can be peace between God and Israel, and God and the land.

A time of great promise is drawing close but when the day dawns which sees the righteous and the wicked separated it will burn up the wicked like straw in an oven; and then...? Keep the faith and obey the rules, says God, and I will send you Elijah the prophet who will reconcile the generations before the 'great and terrible Day of the Lord'.[ccviii] This is different, Elijah – miraculously revived or possibly never dead – is cast as a harbinger and forerunner for the advent of a new age, an age that will see no more wickedness, no more venality, no more strife, an age which we call Messianic.

It is a powerful, if slightly enigmatic ending to the twelve Minor Prophets and, so far as the Hebrew Bible is concerned, the corpus of prophetic literature. The Christian Old Testament canon, however, places the Book of Daniel after that of Ezekiel, firmly placing him with the prophets rather than with the historical books of Ezra-Nehemiah as in the Hebrew canon. In recognition of this, and also the fact that many Jews think of him as a prophet, my final sideways view will be of Daniel.

Chapter 10

Daniel

Key text: The Book of Daniel
Date: ca. 2nd century BCE

Daniel is a character with a long tradition in the earliest Near East. When the ancient city of Ugarit in Syria, on a point marking the closest the Levant gets to the tip of Cyprus, was first excavated by French archaeologists in the late 1920s and early 30s, hundreds of tablets were found written in seven different scripts and four languages.

One of the notable texts to be discovered – dated to the fourteenth century BCE – has been called the Aqhat Epic, which figures an ancient hero called *Dn'il* who is wise and righteous; like some of the biblical prophets *Dn'il* is depicted as caring for widows and orphans, a gentle judge.[ccix] Intriguingly, the book of Ezekiel also refers to this *Dn'il*, calling him Dan'el, and placing him with Noah and Job as righteous and wise men of the past.[ccx]

It is widely believed that this Dan'el is the person on whom the biblical Daniel, described as a senior courtier in Babylon, is based, a decent man with a profound faith in God.

The Book of Daniel is a strange confection: it is written in two languages, Hebrew and Aramaic,[ccxi] a phenomenon differently explained by scholars. It is set in the period when the Babylonian empire came to an end and was succeeded by its conqueror Persia [second half of the 5th century BCE]. Daniel, part of the first Babylonian deportation, is made a ward of the royal court and is thereafter connected to the households of Nebuchadnezzar, Belshazzar and the early Persian kings. The best known stories in the Book of Daniel – the burning fiery furnace of Nebuchadnezzar from which Shadrach, Meshach and Abed-Nego were saved by an angel,[ccxii] the banquet of Belshazzar when writing appears on the wall to announce the ending of the Babylonian Empire,[ccxiii] and Daniel in the lions' den[ccxiv] – are not the summit of the book; that is the series of extraordinary visions that Daniel has which have been and continue to be the focus of fevered analysis trying to tie them to contemporary events.

In one vision he sees four massive and grotesque beasts emerge from the sea,[ccxv] in another a ram with two enormous horns and a goat with one that breaks and is replaced by four.[ccxvi] These visions are explained in the book and it is from these explanations that scholars have concluded that the Book of Daniel should be firmly placed in the second century BCE making it one of the latest books in the Hebrew canon.

The justification for this date is based on the identification of the four horns on the goat with Alexander the Great's generals who created kingdoms and empires on his premature death. Also in this vision a 'holy being' talks about 'the sacrificial cult being suspended and the holy place being abandoned'[ccxvii] which appears to point towards the Seleucid king Antiochus IV Epiphanes who trashed and desecrated the Temple in Jerusalem, its desolation not being ended until the city and Temple were captured by the Jewish army that vanquished the Seleucids, led by their general Judah the Maccabee in 164 BCE.

In addition to the visions there are some other images that have raised Daniel's significance onto a higher plane. In chapter 7 the origin of the childhood vision of God as an old man dressed in white on a throne appears, Daniel describing God as the Ancient of Days on a fiery throne attended by countless angels and minions, presiding as judge over the world.[ccxviii] This image is repeated later in the same chapter enshrining the concept of the Ancient of Days as Judge. Shortly after seeing the Ancient of Days in one vision Daniel has another during the night in which he sees someone like a human being, *bar enash* in Aramaic, meaning son of man, who is presented to the Ancient of Days and is then given everlasting rule over the entire world.[ccxix]

Readers may make an immediate association with the Christian gospels where Jesus is frequently called 'Son of Man', investing this phrase with more significance than its usage in the Hebrew Bible really merits, and the vision itself was interpreted by Christians as God the Father investing God the Son with everlasting dominion over the world and its inhabitants.

Although the Qumran sect responsible for the Dead Sea Scrolls saw Daniel as a prophet, and the Roman Jewish historian Flavius Josephus calls him a 'prophet of good things' in his Antiquities[ccxx] indicating that early Judaism was comfortable with his prophetic status, the Christological use of Daniel and with it his status as a prophet made him less acceptable to the rabbis who are rather grudging about his prophetic credentials.

Nevertheless, for contemporary readers the Book of Daniel as an example not only of great faith but also some wonderful imagery supersedes controversies about meanings and interpretations and remains one of the most intriguing books of the Hebrew Bible.

Postscript

The prophets of Israel lived thousands of years ago. They were ordinary men and women who felt called to do something extraordinary, often at great cost to themselves and their inner lives. Yet they spoke truth to power and stood against the popular will and *mores* of the time.

We who seek messages and teachings from the words of Israel's prophets find plenty that it as relevant now as it was when they were first enunciated, and a reminder of how far we fall short of the irreducible minimums that they expressed for a moral society.

We also find material that sits less comfortably with us; their widespread though not universal misogyny, and the bitter invective against foreign countries and peoples that today we label 'hate speech', and associate with fanatics who couple their words with acts of murder and barbarity described by them as the 'will of God'.

Nevertheless the prophets of Israel have had, and continue to have, a major and overwhelmingly positive influence on Judeo-Christian civilisation and ultimately, when weighed in the balance, remain an abiding stimulus to do well and live right.

Glossary

All Hebrew place and personal names are transliterated according to the standard Sephardi pronunciation of Hebrew

Ba-al	one of the most important deities of the Canaanite pagan pantheon
B.T.	standard abbreviation for the Babylonian Talmud
Chanukkiyah	The nine branched candelabrum lit during the winter festival of Chanukkah, celebrating the liberation and purification of the Jerusalem Temple in the 2nd century BCE
Eshet Zenunim	a seasoned hooker (my translation)
Georg Frederic Handel	German-born British composer, wrote Zadok the Priest as an anthem for the coronation of George II in 1727.
Haftarah	Lit., conclusion, but today standing for the Prophetic reading that follows a reading from the Torah
Ha-neviah	The Prophetess; from a root meaning to prophesy, in its oldest forms of religious ecstasy with or without song and music
Kiryat Ye-arim	Small town to the west of Jerusalem where the Ark of the Covenant resided for twenty years before being taken to Jerusalem by King David
KJV	King James Version
Midrash Aggadah	A collection of biblical commentary and exegesis attributed to the school of the 11th century scholar Moshe Ha-Darshan of Narbonne

Midrash Rabbah	The great corpus of rabbinic exegesis to the Torah and the books of Song of Songs, Ruth, Lamentations, Ecclesiastes and Esther, compiled between the 5th and 12th centuries C.E.
NEB	New English Bible
NJV	New Jewish Version
NRSV	New Revised Standard Version
Schistocerca gregaria	Latin name for the desert locust
Septuagint	The name of the Greek translation of the Hebrew Bible undertaken according to legend over seventy-two days in the city of Alexandria in the 3rd century BCE
Shigyonot	a song evoking excitement through its performance
Sturm und Drang	Storm and Stress/Storm and Drive
Tammuz	Hebrew month, the 4th in the year, usually coinciding with June–July in the secular calendar
Tashlikh	Lit., you will cast, the name of the symbolic jettisoning of sins ceremony held on the afternoon of the first day of the Jewish New Year
The Thirteen Attributes	found in Exodus 34.6–7: 'The Lord, the Lord, a God merciful and gracious, slow to anger, and abounding in steadfast love for the thousandth generation, forgiving iniquity, transgression and sin, yet by no means clearing the guilty, but visiting the iniquity of the parents upon the children and the children's children to the third and the fourth generation.' (NRSV)
Torah	The Five Books of Moses, the standard Hebrew name
Wadi	Dry river bed, Arabic

Suggestions for further reading

Heschel, A.J., The Prophets, Harper Perennial 2001

Brettler, M.Z., Berlin, A., (eds) The Jewish Study Bible, 2nd Edition, Oxford University Press 2014

Wiesel, E., Five Biblical Portraits, University of Notre Dame Press, 1981 (chapters on Elijah, Jonah and Jeremiah)

———— Wise Men and Their Tales: Portraits of Biblical, Talmudic and Hasidic Masters, Schocken Books 2003 (chapters on Isaiah and Hosea)

———— Sages and Dreamers: Biblical, Talmudic, and Hasidic Portraits and Legends, Summit Books 1991 (chapters on Ezekiel and Daniel)

Fishbane, M., The JPS Bible Commentary: Haftarot, Jewish Publication Society 2002 (essays on the prophetic books excerpted in the Haftarah Cycle)

NOTES

i	Exodus 15.20
ii	Numbers 12.1-16
iii	Exodus Rabbah 1.22
iv	Judges 4.6-8
v	Judges 4.5; Judges 5. 1-31
vi	Judges 5.24-27
vii	1 Samuel 1.1-28
viii	1 Samuel 3. 1-14, 19-21
ix	1 Samuel 7.1-2
x	1 Samuel 8.4-5
xi	1 Samuel 8.10-18
xii	1 Samuel 10.1
xiii	1 Samuel 11.14-12.13
xiv	1 Samuel 12.1-25
xv	1 Samuel 13.11-14
xvi	1 Samuel 15.22-23
xvii	1 Samuel 28.4-20
xviii	1 Samuel 28.19
xix	2 Samuel 7.1-3
xx	2 Samuel 7.12-16
xxi	2 Samuel 12.1-12
xxii	2 Samuel 12.14
xxiii	2 Samuel 12.24-25
xxiv	2 Kings 22.14-17
xxv	2 Kings 23.4-20
xxvi	1 Kings 14.6
xxvii	1 Kings 14.7-16
xxviii	1 Kings 22.8,18
xxix	1 Kings 17.8 -24
xxx	1 Kings 18.20-40
xxxi	1 Kings 19.1-2
xxxii	1 Kings 19.9-10, 14
xxxiii	1 Kings 19.15-17
xxxiv	1 Kings 21.7-14
xxxv	1 Kings 21.29
xxxvi	2 Kings 1.2-17
xxxvii	1 Kings 19.19
xxxviii	2 Kings 2.12
xxxix	2 Kings 2.14-15
xl	2 Kings 2.23-24
xli	2 Kings 4.8-37
xlii	2 Kings 5.1-19
xliii	2 Kings 6.5-7
xliv	2 Kings 6.8-23; 2 Kings 7.1-16
xlv	2 Kings 8.7-15; 9.1-14, 30-35
xlvi	2 Kings 13.14-19
xlvii	2 Kings 13.20-21
xlviii	2 Kings 18.13-37; 19.1-7
xlix	2 Kings 19.8-19
l	2 Kings 19.20-28
li	2 Kings 19.29-37

lii	2 Kings 20.1-7
liii	2 Kings 20.16-19
liv	Isaiah 6.1-13
lv	Isaiah 1.10-20
lvi	Isaiah 3.16-26
lvii	Isaiah 13.1-14.7
lviii	Isaiah 13.14-16
lix	Isaiah 14.1-2
lx	Isaiah 19.1-17
lxi	Isaiah 19.18-25
lxii	Isaiah 7.3; 8.1-4
lxiii	Isaiah 20.1-6
lxiv	Isaiah 22.15-25
lxv	Isaiah 22.16; British Museum, acquired 1871
lxvi	Isaiah 11.1-9
lxvii	Isaiah 9.1
lxviii	Isaiah 35.5-6
lxix	Isaiah 7.14
lxx	Isaiah 2.2-3
lxxi	Jeremiah 27.6
lxxii	Isaiah 44.28
lxxiii	Isaiah 45.1-8
lxxiv	Isaiah 47.1-15
lxxv	Jeremiah 1.5
lxxvi	Jeremiah 1.6-8
lxxvii	Jeremiah 1.9
lxxviii	Jeremiah 4.19
lxxix	Jeremiah 5.15
lxxx	Jeremiah 7.1-15
lxxxi	Jeremiah 7.32-8.3
lxxxii	Jeremiah 8.21
lxxxiii	Jeremiah 9.20-21
lxxxiv	Jeremiah 9.23-24
lxxxv	Jeremiah 11.18-23
lxxxvi	Jeremiah 14.13-16
lxxxvii	Jeremiah 19.1-9;20.1-6
lxxxviii	Jeremiah 15.10
lxxxix	Jeremiah 16.1-4
xc	Jeremiah 18.18-23
xci	Jeremiah 19.14-20.2
xcii	Jeremiah 20.3-6
xciii	Jeremiah 20.7,8b,14-15
xciv	Jeremiah 20. 17-18
xcv	Jeremiah 21.1-2
xcvi	Jeremiah 21.3-10
xcvii	Jeremiah 23.11-22
xcviii	Jeremiah 25.27
xcix	Jeremiah 26.12-16

c	Jeremiah 26.20-23
ci	Jeremiah 27.1-22
cii	Jeremiah 30.1-11,17-24
ciii	Jeremiah 28.1-17
civ	Jeremiah 37.17-38.6
cv	Jeremiah 38.7-13
cvi	Jeremiah 39.11-14
cvii	Jeremiah 42.1-17
cviii	Jeremiah 50, 51
cix	Jeremiah 51.59-64
cx	Jeremiah 32.6-15
cxi	2 Kings 17.5-19
cxii	Jeremiah 29.4-9
cxiii	Jeremiah 25.10-14
cxiv	Mark 6.4
cxv	Midrash Aggadah, Numbers 30.15
cxvi	Ezekiel 1.1-21
cxvii	Ezekiel 1.26-28
cxviii	Ezekiel 2.6
cxix	Ezekiel 3.7
cxx	Ezekiel 8.3;24.15-18
cxxi	Ezekiel 38.1-39.16; 40.1-46.24; 45.13-25
cxxii	Ezekiel 16.1-58
cxxiii	Ezekiel 23.1-45
cxxiv	Ezekiel 32.1-32
cxxv	Ezekiel 37.1-14
cxxvi	Hosea 1.1
cxxvii	Hosea 1.2
cxxviii	Hosea 1.3,6,8
cxxix	Hosea 3.1-3
cxxx	Hosea 13.1-14.9
cxxxi	Joel 4.6
cxxxii	Joel 1.11-12,15-20; 2.1-2
cxxxiii	Joel 2.12-14, 2.26-27; Exodus 34.6-7; Jonah 4.2
cxxxiv	Joel 3.1-5
cxxxv	Joel 2.15-27
cxxxvi	Joel 1.4; 2.25
cxxxvii	Amos 1.1
cxxxviii	2 Kings 3.4
cxxxix	1 Samuel 16.11
cxl	Amos 2.6-3.15
cxli	Amos 3.12-4.3
cxlii	Amos 4.1-3
cxliii	Amos 5.14-15
cxliv	Amos 5.19
cxlv	Amos 5.20
cxlvi	Amos 7.2-3,5-6
cxlvii	Amos 7.10-15

cxlviii	Amos 7.16-17
cxlix	Amos 9.7-8
cl	1 Kings 18.2-8
cli	Leviticus Rabbah 18.2
clii	Genesis 36.1-43
cliii	Obadiah vv.10-13
cliv	Obadiah v.14
clv	Psalm 137.7
clvi	2 Kings 14.25
clvii	Jonah 1.1-5
clviii	Jonah 1.7-8
clix	Jonah 1.14,16
clx	Jonah 4.1-2
clxi	Jonah 4.3
clxii	Jonah 4.6-8
clxiii	Jonah 4.9
clxiv	Jonah 4.10-11
clxv	Micah 4.1-3, 6.8
clxvi	Isaiah 2.2-4
clxvii	Micah 4.4
clxviii	Micah 1.2-2.11
clxix	Micah 7.8-10
clxx	Micah 7.19
clxxi	Exodus 34.6-7
clxxii	Nahum 1.2-3
clxxiii	Nahum 2.1-13
clxxiv	Nahum 2.1-3.7
clxxv	Nahum 3.19
clxxvi	Habakkuk 1.2-4
clxxvii	Habakkuk 1.7-8
clxxviii	Habakkuk 1.15-17;2.1
clxxix	Habakkuk 2.2
clxxx	Jeremiah 36.2
clxxxi	Habakkuk 3.1-15
clxxxii	Habakkuk 2.3b; Maimonides, Commentary on the Mishnah, Sanhedrin 10
clxxxiii	Zephaniah 1.2-2.15
clxxxiv	Zephaniah 2.1-15
clxxxv	Zephaniah 1.1
clxxxvi	Zephaniah 2.13-15
clxxxvii	Zephaniah 2.14
clxxxviii	As above
clxxxix	Zephaniah 3.14-20; Genesis 22.17-18
cxc	Haggai 1.13-14
cxci	Haggai 2.23
cxcii	Haggai 1.1, 2.1, 2.10, 2.20
cxciii	Haggai 2.20-23
cxciv	Zechariah 1.9, 12, 13
cxcv	Zechariah 1.8, 2.1,3,5; 3.1-5; 4.1-3; 5.1-2, 5.5-9; 6.1-6

cxcvi   Daniel 8.16; 9.21
cxcvii   Zechariah 14.1-4, 12-15, 16-19
cxcviii   Zechariah 14.21
cxcix   Zechariah 4.6
cc   Zechariah 9.9
cci   Zechariah 13.2-6
ccii   Zechariah 13.5;
cciii   Zechariah 13.4-5; BT Yoma 9b
cciv   Malachi 2.11
ccv   Ezra 10.11
ccvi   Nehemiah 13.3
ccvii   Malachi 3.1-12
ccviii   Malachi 3.23
ccix   The Tale of Aqhat in ANET, ed. James B. Pritchard, pp.118-132
ccx   Ezekiel 14.14, 20; 28.3
ccxi   Daniel 2.4-7.28 is written in Aramaic
ccxii   Daniel 3.13-30
ccxiii   Daniel 5.1-30
ccxiv   Daniel 6.16-25
ccxv   Daniel 7.2-28
ccxvi   Daniel 8.2-26
ccxvii   Daniel 8.11-14
ccxviii   Daniel 7.9-10
ccxix   Daniel 7.13-14
ccxx   Flavius Josephus, Antiquities, 10.11.7.263-268

ABOUT THE AUTHOR

Charles Middleburgh was born and raised in Sussex, on the South Coast of England. At university he completed a BA Hons degree in Biblical Hebrew with Aramaic and Syriac, and a PhD in Targumic studies. He studied for the rabbinate at Leo Baeck College, London, and received Ordination from Rabbi John D Rayner in 1986.

Over a forty-two year career Charles has served Brighton and Hove Progressive Synagogue, Kingston Liberal Synagogue, Harrow and Wembley Progressive Synagogue, the Dublin Jewish Progressive Congregation and Cardiff Reform Synagogue; he helped found a Progressive community in Luxembourg and is the Founder Rabbi of Congregation *Shir HaTzaphon* in Copenhagen. From 1997-2002 he was Executive Director of the Union of Liberal and Progressive Synagogues. In 2015 he was appointed Rabbi Emeritus of the Dublin Jewish Progressive Congregation which he served from 2002 to 2012 and still serves on a part-time basis.

Charles started teaching at Leo Baeck College in 1984 and has been part of the faculty ever since. In 2011 he was appointed Director of Jewish Studies and in 2013 became Dean; he is also Reader in Bible and Jewish Liturgy.

Charles has contributed to each volume of Professor Larry Hoffman's series *Prayers of Awe* (Jewish Lights Publishing) and was Associate Editor of the Liberal Daily, Sabbath and Festival prayer book, *Siddur Lev Chadash*; he was co-editor with Rabbi Dr Andrew Goldstein of the Liberal High Holy Day prayer book, *Machzor Ruach Chadashah*, and together with Rabbi Dr Goldstein has co-edited two anthologies, *High and Holy Days: a Book of Jewish Wisdom* and *A Jewish Book of Comfort* (Canterbury Press).

Charles is a keen wildlife photographer and an ardent conservationist; he has published a collection of poems on the natural world, *Bright and Beautiful*, and contributed poems to *The Hare Book* and *The Fox Book* (Graffeg). He and his wife Gilly currently live in South Wales with their dogs Mottel and Charley.

Printed by Books on Demand GmbH, Norderstedt / Germany